Bread on My Mother's Table

Bread on My Mother's Table

◆

A Danube Swabian Remembers

Ingrid Andor

iUniverse, Inc.

New York Lincoln Shanghai

Bread on My Mother's Table
A Danube Swabian Remembers

iUniverse books may be ordered through booksellers or by contacting:

iUniverse
2021 Pine Lake Road, Suite 100
Lincoln, NE 68512
www.iuniverse.com
1-800-Authors (1-800-288-4677)

Because of the dynamic nature of the Internet, any Web addresses or links contained in this book may have changed since publication and may no longer be valid.

The views expressed in this work are solely those of the author and do not necessarily reflect the views of the publisher, and the publisher hereby disclaims any responsibility for them.

Jules Breton, French, 1827-1906, The Song of the Lark, 1884, oil on canvas, 110.6 x 85.8 cm, Henry Field Memorial Collection, 1894.1033, The Art Institute of Chicago. Photography © The Art Institute of Chicago.

ISBN: 978-0-595-46672-6 (pbk)
ISBN: 978-0-595-90967-4 (ebk)

Printed in the United States of America

This book is dedicated to the memory of

Henry Andor

Helena and Jacob Thoebert

Maria and Peter Deutsch

Eva and Peter Becker

Eva Zettl

Helen Deutsch Walker

Mathias and Katharina Thoebert

Stefan Zettl

*and to all those who have gone before us
to lay the table with bread.*

Danube Swabian Settlement Areas 1683-1945

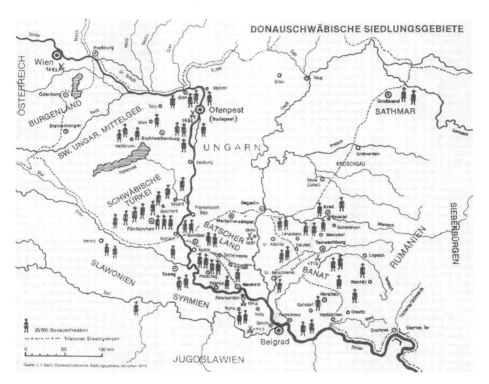

Map of the Danube Swabian settlements in the Batschka and Banat reprinted from the book, *Genocide of the Ethnic Germans in Yugoslavia: 1944-1948,* with permission from the publisher, Danube Swabian Association of the USA.

Contents

List of Photos xi

Acknowledgements xiii

Introduction "I was scared they would see us and we couldn't get away." 1

Part I   In the Camp in Kruschiwl

Chapter 1 "They can take everything away from me again, except bread." 9

Chapter 2 "Leave your houses unlocked and heated and put fresh bread on the table." 13

Chapter 3 "People hid things in the ground." 19

Chapter 4 "We made ourselves look ugly to escape the shoulders." . 25

Chapter 5 "As field workers, we got a little extra bread." 31

Chapter 6 "When you are a teenager, you feel invincible." 35

Chapter 7 "Wenn mir durch Gakowa geht und net ausgelacht wird ..." 41

Chapter 8 "Once I was sitting at a riverbank crying ..." 53

Part II   Deportation to Russia

Chapter 9 "Na, na, Jacob." 65

Chapter 10 "I remember him going in the pantry six or seven times a night ..." 73

Chapter 11 "Was Ota a Nazi?" 79

Chapter 12 "Take this bread and eat of it." 85

Chapter 13 "We didn't get very much food to eat in the camp." . . .99

Part III   *From Refugees to Immigrants ~ The Journey to America*

Chapter 14 "I was raised to get by on a very little." 109

Chapter 15 "For my mother, it was bread. For my father, it was being educated." 125

Chapter 16 "I remember this one fur coat they sent me." 141

Part IV   *The End Peace ~ The Heal of the Bread*

Chapter 17 "Would you go back?" 153

Chapter 18 "Don't be ashamed of who you are." 159

Afterword "Yes, Mother, I remember." 165

About the Author 171

Notes 173

Bibliography 175

List of Photos

Picture 1

1) A typical Krushiwl homestead.

Picture 2

2) Maria Andor in Austria.

Picture 3

3) An artist's depiction of breadbaking in Kruschiwl.

Picture 4

4) Henry Andor with Sissy.

Picture 5

5) Katharina Burlem and Maria Andor.

Picture 6

6) The refugees in Austria.

Picture 7

7) Katharina Burlem.

Picture 8

8) Maria Andor and Christine Kiefer.

Picture 9

9) Christine Kiefer as a child and her family in Kernei.

Picture 10

10) Helena Deutsch in Kruschiwl.

Picture 11

11) Jacob and Helena Thoebert.

Picture 12

12) Peter Becker and Jacob Thoebert.

Picture 13

13) Jakob Zettl and his family in Kruschiwl.

Picture 14

14) Rosalia and Adam Szettele on their wedding day in Kruschiwl.

Picture 15

15) Citizenship Day photo of Maria Andor and family.

Picture 16

16) Henry Andor as a young immigrant.

Picture 17

17) Henry Andor, Jr., Ingrid Andor, and Katharina Szettele Gronner as children.

Picture 18

18) Henry Andor, Jr. on his wedding day.

Picture 19

19) Maria Andor with baby daughter, Ingrid.

Picture 20

20) Maria Andor in Sindelfingen, Germany.

Picture 21

The author and her family, 2007.

Acknowledgements

My sincere thanks go to all of the Donauschwaben, who shared their unique stories with me, and to the historian and writer, Alfred-Maurice de Zayas, for his extensive work on the Danube Swabian expulsion history.

My thanks go also to Carol Dovi O'Dwyer for always believing in me as a writer and for gently insisting that this story be published.

A typical Danube Swabian house in Kruschiwl.

Introduction

*"I was scared they would see us and we couldn't get away.
That's why I wanted to leave so fast. I didn't want to be there.
It's not a place you ever want to go."*
Maria Andor

I was eight years old the first time I saw my mother cry. I was sitting in the back seat of a rented Opel Kadett and we—my father, mother and six-year-old brother—had just pulled into the ghost town of Kruschiwl, Yugoslavia, the town my mother grew up in. Kruschiwl is one of the stops on what I now jokingly refer to as our "roots" trip, when we visited the places where my parents were born. Today it is Mother's turn to go back into time.

From the back seat of the car I see my mother's and father's faces in close profile, framed by the small windshield that overlooks a desolate vista of dusty dirt road. Outlining the road are crumbling skeletons of houses with bricks strewn about, haphazardly lining what was once the main street of a neat-as-a-pin farming village.

"Turn around, Henry," my mother cries out suddenly. "Just turn around. Let's leave now."

Her head is moving rapidly from left to right and her voice cracks with tears and rides a wave of desperation that I have never heard—before or since—from this incredibly predictable, stable, and not prone-to-emotional-outbursts woman.

My father, weary from driving hours through Germany and Hungary and smiling broadly at every Checkpoint Charley as he handed out 19-cent Bic pens to much fanfare behind the Iron Curtain, has a pleading, soothing, cooing sound to his voice, like a pigeon not ready to leave its roost after just coming home from a long day in flight.

"Mary, please. Just a little while," he begs. "We'll just take a few pictures and then we'll go. Please, Mary. Please."

I look around and I am confused about the need for taking pictures and startled by my mother's unusual reaction. There are no purple mountain majesties here. Kruschiwl is an ugly name for a town. And on this day in 1963 it is not a pretty place.

1

Gone are the whitewashed settler's baroque homes that were passed lovingly from generation to generation for 200 years since they were originally homesteaded in the 1700's. In the place of these once large, rectangular homes that bordered and faced each other on both sides of the street are the ruins of houses, like old dinosaur bones overgrown with weeds. Only one broken down wall—a remnant of the main living quarters—is left on Uncle Adam's old house, and there is nothing here of the huge courtyard or the livestock quarters. For that matter, there are no neighing, mooing, or crowing sounds to herald our arrival.

We get out of the car, the smell of dust and baked summer earth in my nose. The overgrowth is everywhere, licking up the jagged walls. Everything is that dead-looking brown-beige, the color of New Mexico desert in August. It is hard for me to imagine that my mother's family once lived here on this main street, this desolate place where we now stood, and they farmed land, well over 100 acres, that was located out in the fields, away from the town center. There are no remnants on this road for my toes to stub on of the railroad tracks that once held the flat bed trolleys that farmers loaded with corn, grain, and sugar beets to market at harvest time. There is nothing here that remotely recalls a bountiful harvest. No waving rows of corn or wheat in the distance beckon me to a game of hide-and-seek in the countryside. This beige, dry, overgrown, wild, untended place bears no resemblance to what was once an orderly farming community.

Suddenly, a lone, curious Serbian woman, anxious to be in the photographs, appears and poses against the cracked walls of what my mother recognizes as her Uncle Jakob's old house. She slinks about in the distance, following us like a cat, as my mother squints through her tears at what is left of her old neighborhood and its silent, childhood places. We take a few more sorry pictures, my father gives the Serbian woman a Bic pen, and we clamber back into the cramped dusty white Opel. Except for the initial sound of the gears rapidly changing as my father speeds our escape, it is strangely quiet in the car for a long time, and I listen to my mother's ragged breaths slowly calm to longer and longer intervals as we get farther and farther away.

My mother tells me later—over 30 years later when the unrelenting memory of seeing my mother's first tears led me finally to ask about her uncharacteristic reaction—that her old town fell under such disrepair because the partisans—Tito's communist freedom fighters—who were given the homes when the townspeople were driven out to concentration camps, did not stay to provide the proper upkeep. The homes were haunted, they said, filled with the ghosts of hunger, disease, and death. Most chose not to stay to enjoy their stolen gifts. In the end, the land itself, as it always does when left to its own devices, turned against them and lay fallow.

Why did she cry? Was it because this dreary Kruschiwl was so different from the living, thriving farming community it once was when she was a girl in the late 30's?

"Not *r*eally," she tells me, rolling the *r* like she always does.

"No, I was scared they would see us and we couldn't get away. That's why I wanted to leave so fast. I didn't want to be there; it's not a place you ever want to go. I told my sister the same thing. Just don't ever go there. There is nothing there to see."

◆   ◆   ◆

Of course, I had to go there. And I picked a wonderful way to do it. My journey back to Kruschiwl involved my bailing from a stable, yet unfulfilling, corporate job in mid-career, taking a side trip to San Miguel de Allende, a peaceful colonial silver city in Mexico where my purpose to write became clear, and returning three weeks later to throw myself headlong into the turbulent sea of uncharted memories. In the process, I found myself questioning the round, hazel eyes of my mother, while sitting across from her at the kitchen table, while hovering over her at the sink, and while riding with her in her big white Chrysler Concorde, and even while sitting beside her on the elevated trains in Chicago.

When I returned from Mexico, I brought my mother a bolillo in hopes that it would help to build a bridge to her past. She ate the bolillo, but still she was appalled.

◆   ◆   ◆

One Night in May, 1997

"Why do you want to do this? Why?"

My mother glares at me with exasperation from her roost at the kitchen table, her game of Solitaire momentarily abandoned, and musters up her most optimistic and straightforward advice.

"Just forget about writing this book and go back to work. It will never be published."

Well-accustomed to the discomfort of my mother's well-worn negativity, I exhale sharply and take the bait instead.

"Now why would you say a thing like that?"

"Because the people that own the publishing companies will not want this story told."

My mother believes in a pecking order among victims of World War II. As an ethnic German expellee, she knows that she is an unpopular victim of a hidden holocaust, and she does not believe that the world is ready to accept or acknowledge Germans as victims.

I disagree. The land of shadows, silence, and denial are the places where stories are born. More than that, I needed to know who she was and what happened to her in October, 1944.

Her hazel eyes beam unwaveringly into my brown ones and she delivers the torpedo she hopes will finally discourage me from my folly.

"No one wants to know anything about this except from the Jews."

I return her unwavering gaze and instead reply defiantly, "I'm writing the book anyway. I have to. And I need you to help me."

PART I
In the Camp in Kruschiwl

While the world was condemning Nazi war crimes at the Nuremberg trials, Hitler's expulsion atrocities were being emulated and practiced on ethnic Germans. The vast majority of these Germans, called *Donauschwaben*, or Danube Swabians, were apolitical farmers, with ancestral roots in eastern Europe over 200 years old.

As a result of the agreement reached by the Allies at the Yalta and Potsdam conferences, Russian and partisan soldiers occupied the ethnic German towns along the Danube, and from late 1944 until 1948, expelled approximately 15 million Danube Swabians from their homelands in Yugoslavia, Romania, Hungary, Czechoslovakia, East Prussia, and Syrmia. The Danube Swabians were dispossessed of their homes, farms, and citizenship rights. Prior to their expulsions, they were interned in concentration camps that were erected in their own towns.

There were 86 exclusively German and 332 predominately German communities spread across the Batschka and Banat, agricultural regions within the Danube Basin, encompassing Romania, Hungary, and Yugoslavia. Kruschiwl, one of the exclusive German villages in the Batschka, was located in the northern part of Yugoslavia, in the Pannonian Lowlands, directly northwest of Belgrade. In the fall of 1944, Kruschiwl, like its neighboring villages of Rudolfsgnad, Gakowa, Mitrovica, and Molidorf, was transformed into a concentration camp. Those unfortunate to not escape the camps died there of illness and starvation and were buried in unmarked, mass graves.

Of the 500,000 Danube Swabians that were in Yugoslavia, it is estimated that approximately 350,000 escaped and resettled, 31,000 died in the war, and 55,000 died in partisan-run camps. Approximately 30,000 survived. One of the survivors, Maria Andor, is my mother.

Maria Andor in Austria.

"They can take everything away from me again, except bread. I can live on bread alone. Just bread."

Maria Andor

Maria

My mother, Maria, is a *breadhead*. That's what I call her. I tease my mother about it all the time. She especially likes freshly baked loaves of white French or Italian bread, and I've never seen her turn away from a hearty rye, either. She's not a fan of sourdough or fancy vegetable or herb concoctions. For a purist like her, it's the basic European, right-out-of-the-oven-without-butter-even piece of bread. It's the crisp light crust and the warm yeast dough that satisfies her craving.

"They can take everything away from me again," she asserts fervently, "except bread."

She is a pack rat, too. She cannot bear to throw a single thing away: another side effect of being enslaved in a labor camp as a teenager and having everything taken away from her. She is a seeker and finder of the best certificate of deposit rates in town. A baker. A lover of food and leftovers that fill her refrigerator and freezer for months in the shape of silver foil moon rocks. Her ample belly bears witness to the fact that she will never be hungry again.

She is a dancer of polkas and waltzes, with a broad smile fixed upon her jovial round face. See her spinning and stomping on the wood floors at the Donauschwaben picnics at Lake Villa. She is a lover of mindless musicals. Dramas have never interested her, especially when her day-to-day existence was once lived as a life-or-death proposition.

Today there are no empty stomachs: no wanting for anything. There is always more than enough to eat and then some more squirreled away for a rainy day, sewn into the lining of one of her dead husband's suits—a trick she learned long ago to hide valuables from demanding soldiers.

She learned other tricks then, too. Like at night when she snuck out of the camps to beg for food, or when she tried to go to another camp to check on friends and family members. When caught by the guards and asked what camp she was coming from, she told them where she wanted to go so they would take her there. She became very clever and evasive. This is the place where she learned how to perfect the vague answer: the answer that reveals nothing useful. This is why I have to ask her a question three or four times before I get an elliptical answer at best.

She is a gardner, having perfected the art of the razor-sharp edging of her lawn. She can trim the bushes that adorn the base of the step railings of her ranch house into flat table tops, capable of holding an entire tea set. She is a farmer's daughter and knows how to grow beautiful tomatoes and Hungarian peppers. What a way she has with hostas that skirt the base of her pine trees like ruffled slips that show under a party dress.

At dawn see her singing and marching into the fields with other teenaged girls under armed partisan guard to harvest wheat and vegetables until dusk, from one field to another. At night see her sleeping, tired and disheveled with so many others on the straw-covered floor of an old barn. See the rats that skitter about over bare legs scratched from working in the fields all day. Smell the unwashed bodies, and hear the keening of the women when the drunk partisan guards begin rustling through the straw, searching for women for their night revelry.

See her as a vagabond, a refugee. See her trudging along, walking with her mother and sister. In 1947, after almost three years in the labor camps, the partisans began turning a blind eye to the many camp prisoners escaping the camps. Some of the guards could even be bribed to help them cross the border at night into Hungary. The "mules of Mexico" were there, called the White Guards.

See her safely to Hungary; see her crossing the border only four kilometers away. But she would not stay there long before the soldiers came to Hungary and her family was uprooted again. The communists loaded everyone up in wagons, took over the town, and moved the Germans to Austria or Germany. She went with her family to Salzburg.

See her in government housing at Fierstenfeld. Wooden barracks filled to bursting with displaced people like her from around the world. Poles. Czechs. Jews. Her life as a refugee began in this camp for displaced persons: barns which had once housed the German army and their horses. There wasn't much food in Austria or Germany then, either. Europe was in a shambles, and her days there were numbered as well.

See her like many of the Danube Swabians, still envious and jealous of the Jews who have become the world's most popular victims of World War II. Feel the result of deep-seated envy and tongue-tied frustration living in a world where a German victim is an oxymoron.

"We died, too," she says, and the television screen flashes off on the latest Holocaust program.

Unser täglich Brot

Artist's depiction of breadbaking in Kruschiwl.

"Leave your houses unlocked and put fresh bread on the table."
Orders from a partisan guard

October, 1944

Two weeks before Tito's partisans came, my mother was in the kitchen making bread with her grandmother. Happily kneading dough on the kitchen table, punching in the warm and sticky sponginess, she heard the sound of the Russian army marching through the center of town, sounding out the drumbeat of a new regime. These Russians had helped Tito to drive the German army out of Belgrade and were now being used to liberate all of Yugoslavia as a communist nation. All ethnic German minorities, like the community my mother had been born to, were to be expelled from their homes and given as gifts of slave labor to the partisan liberators who followed.

She was a farmer's daughter, born to Danube Swabians that had lived and settled the land in the Yugoslavian Batschka. The inhabitants of the Batschka found themselves caught between the snares of fascism and communism, peacefully making bread and tending to their harvests. In October 1944, the harvest would be a bitter time and the yearly slaughter would take on a terrible toll in human suffering. Belongings, livestock, homes, crops, and lives would suddenly be taken over. In the time it takes to make a loaf of bread, the life of a 15-year-old girl would change forever.

◆   ◆   ◆

To the Danube Swabians, bread was more than bread. It represented life itself. A full belly, a successful harvest, a life well lived, a farmer's job well done. All of these things and more. A connection to the earth and the mouth that is infinite and visceral.

My mother still has it: this devotion to bread. After church on Sundays she stands at the kitchen counter, an apron covering her dress, the fresh loaf of

Gonella bread lies there with its white belly having been exposed to her knife, the freshly cut end piece quickly disappearing into her hungry mouth. If the Holy Trinity were a square, for my mother it would be God the Father, God the Son, God the Holy Spirit, and God the Freshly Baked Loaf of Bread. Right out of the oven, put some butter on it, some bacon fat, some sugar, or go all out with the sugar and some rum, or just nothing at all but the bread itself.

Bread. Bread. Bread. Bread is bigger than life. Bread is more than enough when there is nothing. Bread is all there ever is sometimes. A reason for waking. A reason for working. A reason for living. Bread is a place she's always known. Bread is Kruschiwl. Fifteen years old at the kitchen table watching the bread cool and waiting for that first slice to fill her up and make her complete. Leave her the bread from the place of her birth to fill her up and make her whole again.

Then, like now, there is always bread on my mother's table.

Bread was *the* staple in the Danube Swabian diet. It was so important, necessary, and loved as a mainstay that virtually every home had an oven in the back of the house dedicated solely to the baking of the bread. From the time she was a young girl, my mother watched her mother and her grandmother participate in this weekly ritual in which four or five loaves were baked.

The bread was made with white flour, always white and never rye or whole wheat. A few other ingredients—water, salt, and yeast—were added to the white flour. There was nothing unusual about the recipe; it was even quite bland, were it not for an interesting twist in the preparation that made the bread so unique.

Bread dough was kneaded by hand and prepared into rounds about six-to-eight inches in diameter. Right before the rounds were placed in the oven, the top of the round would be pulled back and up, like bread taffy, and then folded over to form a lid on the remainder of the round. This folding technique made the bread bake up to an immense height.

The baking oven was fueled by corn stalks. Nothing ever goes to waste on a farm, not even corn stalks. The cows eat off all the leaves, and then the stalks are left to dry. Once dry, the stalks become fuel for the baking oven, burning hot and long in an oven not powered by gas or electricity. When the baking oven, or *Bak Ofa*, was nice and hot, the dough was placed on greased, three-legged stools which were slid into the oven with a long-handled baker's spatula. The bread baked beautifully on the special stool, and as it baked it rose to a nice, golden-encrusted top hat.

Almost every family in town had a *Bak Ofa*. The few families who did not have the means to afford one, or those who just didn't want to heat up the back of the house with bread baking in summer, would give the ingredients or the prepared dough rounds to the town's baker. Either way, everyone had bread. Come hell or high water, everyone had bread.

When the able-bodied were deported to Russia as slave labor, all they received to eat was bread. One piece in the morning and one at night. But this bread was not their beloved Danube Swabian white bread. It was 800 grams of soggy, half-cooked bread that sat like a wet pile of rags in their stomachs. There was nothing of the sun or the fields or the warmth of their youth in this bread. This bread evoked no memories of sifting cool, silky softness through the fingers or being taught by their grandmothers the recipe of their ancestors. This bread had a heaviness of water and sorrow and stuck in the throat when swallowed and fell heavily like a stone.

When my Uncle Adam was captive in the labor camp in Siberia, he received only two pieces of bread a day. Sometimes he would wait to eat both pieces at one sitting. How could he wait with that soggy piece of bread in his back pocket, working all day with hunger pangs circling his middle like a snake and stabbing him in the side?

Those, like my mother, who were interned in the concentration camp in Kruschiwl and other neighboring towns were forced to trade their beloved Danube Swabian bread for moldy corn bread and bug-infested, watery pea soup. Corn bread is pig swill to the Danube Swabians who had feasted on fresh white bread all their lives. Most of them who survived the horrors of captivity in the camps and the illness brought on by the poor diet will tell you, bar none, that they do not eat corn bread to this day. Corn bread is the food of slaves, of captivity, of sickness, and despair. Corn bread is never served on my mother's table.

◆   ◆   ◆

Snare drums signaled the advancement. You heard the drums before the marching of the boots. After the Russian army moved through town, all of you knew the German army was defeated, pushed back and away. Any protection you may have imagined was stripped away. With each trill of the drum snares, your hearts filled with an increasing dread. You were so vulnerable. And many of your men, like your cousin Adam, had been drafted to fight in the Hungarian and German armies. And there you were, stonily gazing out of the window of the home you would call your own for the last time, with your hands elbow deep in dough and a smudge of flour on your forehead.

Soon after the Russians moved on, Tito's partisans followed. They took control, occupying the town and cordoning it off with barbed wire, placing armed sentries on the perimeter. The townspeople were told to gather at the town square and were given these orders:

"Leave your houses unlocked and heated, and put fresh bread on the table."

So, there you are with your grandmother again in the kitchen making bread. Little do you know that this bread you will never eat. This is the bread that will welcome your captors into your home.

Henry Andor with Sissy.

"People hid things in the ground. Jewelry, money and such.
I was just a young girl then and I didn't have much to hide."

Maria Andor

Before the partisans came, the townspeople went into the cornfields and buried their jewelry and other valuables. They got word that the partisans were coming and they went out at night, their shovels glinting in the moonlight, and they dug small holes all over their fields. They took their rings, watches, necklaces, bracelets, money—whatever they had of any value. They dug small holes and into the ground it went, wrapped neatly in old newspaper, laid carefully in a small cardboard box.

The people went at night. They dug quietly. So quietly that their neighbors didn't even know where they were digging. They remembered their hiding places. Three rows down. One row up. Ten paces to the right. Like a mathematical formula, a combination only they would remember. Three plus one plus ten to the right. You never knew when it might come in handy. Three plus one plus ten could equal bread, an end to hunger, the saving of a life in the camps. A train ticket to freedom. You never knew. It was better to keep the hiding place a secret from everyone.

My mother learned to hide things. Even though she didn't have much as a girl of 15 when the partisans occupied Kruschiwl, she watched her parents protect what they had. She watched her mother sew valuables into the hems of her skirts and her father clutch a small box in his hand as he hitched up the horses at night.

◆   ◆   ◆

After my father died in 1978, I discovered that she hid money in his old suits, which still hung in the closet next to her blouses and skirts. Once I saw her pull a $20 bill out of an inside breast pocket for groceries. She stores things in her hall closet like a squirrel with acorns in the fall. Old cereal. Boxes of Bugles. Stale potato chips and low sodium Bavarian pretzels. Plastic Tupperware containers. Mostly empty but sometimes filled to the brim with cookies. Everything is neatly stacked but crowded in, edge to edge, in my mother's closet. Boxes and old telephone directories, the reusable, red Valentine's heart box from chocolates she bought in 1985. And, always a half a can of mixed nuts at easy arm's reach.

At some point, she started hiding her heart. She found a hole and buried it deep inside. I don't know if it was when our sweet, little fawn-like Chihuahua, Sissy, died, or when my father passed away from a sudden heart attack. Or, maybe, the hiding started even earlier, when she was just a girl and had to leave her mother for the first time and walk into the fields in spring, not to return again until fall. Maybe it began when her mother hid her and her sister in the haylofts to keep them safe from the partisan soldiers, and they crouched together, listening to the whistling of stray bullets over their heads.

◆   ◆   ◆

I was 13 years old the second time I saw my mother cry. She had just learned from my father that Sissy had wandered into the street and was killed instantly by a passing car. My father brought Sissy home in a discarded newspaper, and while he and my brother buried her in the backyard, I sat at the piano, staring blurry-eyed at the jagged black and white keyboard and listened to her sob. In intermittent bursts, like rain showers, she cried for a week.

She adored that dog. There is a peculiar picture I can no longer find of her sitting on a green and white checkered lounge chair at LaBaugh Woods. The picture was taken on the occasion of a family picnic, something we used to do a lot in the summers when I was a girl. My mother is dressed in shorts and has her legs drawn up; she's wearing white rhinestone-studded sunglasses, and the dog is perched peacefully between her legs.

She was crazy for that dog, if you can say the word 'crazy' in relationship to my mother. My mother isn't wild crazy about anything, and she's attached to few things nowadays, except her stubborn independence. My fox terriers look like adorable stuffed animals, especially when they get a shower and a shave, but she skirts around them protectively, admiring them as if they were ancient antiquities on display at the Field Museum.

When my father died, there were no more men to enter her life. At age 51, she found another hole and buried another piece of her heart.

"Don't you want to date, Mom?" I'd ask.

"Who wants the hassle?" she'd reply.

"Marriage must not be all it's cracked up to be," I'd muse.

She kept them away. A force field protects the place where she once had her passion.

As I grew up, I was taught to hide my feelings.

"No one wants to hear it," they'd say when I'd get my feelings hurt and gear up for a good sobbing.

"If you're going to cry, go away and take care of it. We don't want to see you cry."

I got into the habit of going into the pink bathroom just outside my bedroom door and having emotional outbursts with a variety of imaginary people in the mirror and many who sat around the tub. We had long, drawn out, frustratingly tearful meetings. The nameless, faceless ones always had something good to say to help me vent and calm down.

My parents wanted to protect me. They were always trying to protect me. Sending me to private schools. Imploring me to date only German boys. Begging me to go to a Catholic college in the city.

"We'll buy you a car if you go to Loyola."

They dangled their carrot temptingly, but still I refused.

They wanted to watch over me. Closely. They didn't want me to be vulnerable to anyone or anything they didn't understand. If an enemy could discern my feelings, if I showed them *on my sleeve*—perish the thought—I could be rudely taken advantage of. I was raised to interact with people the way others negotiate an automobile sale. Cooly. Dispassionately. Respectfully. And above all, quietly, and with grave distrust.

I'm not sure when my mother started to hide from me. Maybe it was after the nervous breakdown I suffered during my second semester at the University of Illinois at Champaign-Urbana. I made the mistake of showing her an incomprehensible weakness. My first chance away from home and I failed to cope without their vigilant watch. From that moment on I became suspect. I was no longer to be trusted. It's been well over 20 years now, and if I so much as exhibit any spirited behavior she perceives as erratic, I will see that peculiar glazed look in her eye and get the standard withdrawal as she turns away to the wonders of the kitchen sink.

"There's nothing I can say," she mutters into the soapy water. "You'll do what you want anyway."

And she still can't stand it when I cry.

She hides shamelessly from me as she does from dogs and men and anything she once held dear. We are all in the realm now of that which can change, leave, or disappoint her. We are in that place across the border that the moat was built upon. Far away in a cornfield is a hiding place where my mother's heart lies—a place she alone can find under the light of a very full moon.

Katharina Burlem and Maria Andor.

"We made ourselves look ugly to escape the soldiers.
We put flour in our hair and dressed like old women.
We pulled babushkas over our eyes to hide at night and
when we worked in the fields outside .
Anything to keep the soldiers away."
Christine Kiefer

June 30, 1997

I am on my way to rendezvous with Maria for our yearly pilgrimage to the Taste of Chicago. At the Belmont stop of the Howard line, I queue up at the doors to switch trains. Something compels me to look south when I step off the train, and everyone else dissolves when I see her cheerful face.

My mother is, well, there's no other way to say it, cute. She's adorable. A real standout in the crowd. At 5'2", she's a little hefty in the middle in an attractive way, and the light catches her strawberry blond hair, which is always beautifully coiffed. She has been wearing her hair short in the back and away from her face with a sweep off to the right for as long as I can remember; it was probably 35 years ago when she gave up her French twist and cut her hair. My father wasn't happy about it. She's got a nice, friendly round face, a pretty smile with these small square teeth that love to chew on chicken bones, and very soft, round, hazel eyes. And, she has the most beautiful, peach-colored complexion in the summer-time. What a beauty she is. We don't look at all alike. I'm my father's daughter with dark brown hair and brown eyes.

Laughing and delighted to see her, I rush over to her like I always do these days and give her a big hug and kiss.

"What are you doing here?" I ask incredulously. "We were supposed to meet at State and Lake."

"I don't know ... I just got confused or something and got off here."

The ride was probably taking too long. She doesn't like being cooped up for long periods of time.

"What a great place for it, huh?"

We are laughing about our good fortune to be able to ride the rest of the way together, and when the Ravenswood train comes along again, I urge her back on and we settle into a double seat where we can get a good look at the grafitti-covered rooftops of the city rushing by in the windows across from us. At this moment, with my mother sitting comfortably to my left, I am feeling happy and playful, and I want very much to know about a time when my mother felt the same way.

"So, tell me, Mom," I begin, "what do you remember about being a child? What kind of toys did you play with in Kruschiwl?"

"Nothing special, really."

There's that rolling 'r' again and that *nothing really,* which signals to me there's definitely more to come. Thankfully, she'll never get rid of her German accent; it's part of her charm. I wait a beat and am rewarded when a warm flush of recollection appears in her eyes. Her face lights up and she warms to her subject, by turns delighted, charmed, and puzzled by my late-blooming interest. As the Ravenswood train moves along on its track downtown, my mother takes me on a journey back in time to a small farming village in eastern Europe.

"Sometimes, toys came to Kruschiwl loaded on the back or pulled in the wagon of the town's peddler, Hans. We called him *Billiger Hans* (Bargain John) because of all the bargains he brought us. He came from time to time with all sorts of odds and ends strapped around his waist and on his back. He brought all sorts of things that we didn't have, like shoelaces and combs," she confides.

Once he even came by horse and buggy carrying a swing set in his hold. But my mother reassures me that her swing set, although far less elaborate, was just as much fun; it was a simple board with holes on the sides for two ropes to be tied to a tree. As she talks, I try to picture her flying from a tree, flying free with the sun in her eyes and billowy clouds drifting in the summer sky overhead.

Manufactured toys, like the swing set that Hans once brought, were not plentiful in Kruschiwl, Yugoslavia, in the late 30's. Instead, as in all agrarian towns, children learned to be naturally creative, finding toys everywhere, dotting the landscape.

There is beauty in stones. In the simple stones you find on a country road or on the beach. Stones and shells dredged up from the lake floor by the tides and made smooth by the hand of erosion: like a parent's touch, both loving and harsh. My mother played a game with perfectly rounded, small stones she would hunt for, and with marbles, too.

I close my eyes and imagine her sitting with her circle of girlfriends. It is her turn to throw out the stones from a cup, and then at first to pick up one stone, then two at a time, then three and four, until all are picked up, or her small hands cannot hold anymore and she drops a stone and relinquishes her turn to the next girl in line. She prefers to play with the stones instead of marbles. The smoother, rounder stones are easier to handle. They don't roll as far away as the marbles do, with their slick, glassy surface. With the stones, it is easier to keep your turn and win the game. This Yugoslavian game of pickup sticks, or jacks, is played for hours on end, until it is time to go in to help grandmother with the cooking or the baking of the bread.

Because she is watched by her grandparents during the day while her parents work in the fields, she learns to entertain and charm them with songs and dances. They sit around the table calling out their favorites and she happily obliges. When she is older, about 12, she starts to play card games with the adults, a past-time she never outgrows. They play games with strange, foreign-sounding names like Mariasch, Lorus, and Koenig Im Eck (King in a Corner). At night she reads stories and plays Miele with her younger sister: a game in which she pushes beans around on a board.

"What were your birthday parties like?" I ask.

"We didn't celebrate birthdays as much as we celebrated name days," she informs me. "We were given the names of saints and we celebrated on their feast days."

"The biggest festivals of all were the Kirchweih festivals. Kirchweih festivals were country fairs that celebrated the founding, or the birthday, of the church. Every town had a church and each church had its feast day, or birthday. Everyone from the town would attend. It was like a founder's day picnic and country fair all wrapped up in one. The food was good and plentiful. The townspeople danced and wore traditional ethnic costumes. Both the children and the adults looked forward to Kirchweih. People would come and set up games like ring toss and stuff like that for the children to play. The town's peddler, Billiger Hans, would usually show up during Kirchweih."

My mother doesn't tell me, but later, my aunt's voice on the cassette tape from Hawaii, does. According to my Aunt Kathy, my mother was a bit of a tom-boy. She liked things that held an element of adventure or danger about them, like playing hide-and-seek in the barn between the cows and the horses. Instead, my mother tells me that she played with *dolls*.

Like all children with a sense of imagination and not many manufactured, store-bought toys, my mother was able to use her creativity to fashion an intriguing game of *house*. The first item, the most obvious, was the easiest to obtain. An old dried-up corn husk could be found anywhere near the pig sty or tossed neatly in the barn. Now to scurry in the grass near the base of the fruit trees. An old short twig could be found there and broken down into a stick. Now tie it like a crossbar over the corn husk to resemble arms. On this makeshift body frame, a *dress* is hung—pieces of old rags or remnant material, or even cutouts from an old newspaper. A corn husk doll is born. Now off we go to make some furniture.

Scampering around in the fields, the girls are searching for what they call *gletta*—the kind of prickly burrs you find sticking to your beach blanket and in the dog's beard. The girls spend afternoons in the fields, stooping down and gathering up burrs by the handfuls in their aprons. For days they collect them, and when they have enough, they gather together in a circle and begin to make furniture for the doll's house. The burrs are good to use because they stick together easily and you can shape them into chairs and couches and beds. My mother's thumb and index finger squeeze together and push out as she talks, and I know her fingers still remember how it feels.

The girls agree amongst themselves to make different pieces of furniture. These burrs, these Leggos of the 30's, are small and oval and sharp with pointy quills. After a day in the fields making furniture, with butterflies flying about, the girls' little fingertips are pink and a little sore from their play. The girls don't even consider it. These inconsequential childhood pricks pale in comparison to the later horrors they would experience as teenagers and young women in the concentration camps.

When the partisans took over the Danube Swabian towns, they lost no time in establishing control and creating a hostile and fearful environment. They began by liquidating all of the influential members of the community. The mayor, members of the town council, merchants, and teachers were taken into buildings and stabbed to death. The men in the community, who were deemed well-to-do capitalists, were marched out of town to dig their own graves, prior to being shot. The remaining able-bodied men were deported to Russia.

With most of the men out of the way, the partisans were free to bully the remaining women and children. Young, beautiful, blonde-haired Danube Swabian women were taken from their families and placed in a brothel, in a compound at Pancevo, across the river from Belgrade. Ultimately, they all became infected with syphilis, and those still alive, approximately 150 women, were taken into a remote pasture and shot to death. The women left in the camps, those lucky to be born brunette, like my mother, were forced to dodge the advances of their partisan guards.

The childhood artists grow up to be creative with costumes and disguise.

My mother's friend Christine tells me, "We made ourselves look ugly to escape the soldiers. We put flour in our hair and dressed like old women. We pulled babushkas over our eyes to hide at night and when we worked in the fields outside. Anything to keep the soldiers away. But some soldiers could still separate the old from the young and tell the difference from behind."

My mother tells me she was never raped in the camps. But I am not sure. She admits to having escaped rather close calls. Once a soldier tried to blackmail her. He caught her cutting up a bicycle tire so she could make soles for her shoes. If she would have sex with him, he wouldn't say anything about the ruined tire. She flatly refused, called his bluff, and somehow got away with it.

The second time she and her friend Viktoria were asked to accompany two soldiers to an abandoned farm.

"That time I thought I wasn't going to get away. But then I saw this older woman."

She desperately pleaded with her to go with them, and the woman agreed to pose as their mother.

"What happened when you got to the farm?"

"Nothing."

"Nothing?" I ask incredulously.

"Ja. Nothing. The soldiers began arguing with each other."

Why didn't they rape all three of you? What stopped them? Was it the force of your personality or your spontaneous creativity that saved you?

◆   ◆   ◆

And afterwards, with her clothing disheveled and her innocence destroyed, a young girl sits tearfully in the fields, picking burrs from the apron of her skirt, a childhood game of house the farthest thing from her mind.

The refugees in Austria. Photo includes Katharina Burlem, Jacob Thoebert, Adam Szettele, Peter Deutsch, Jakob Zettl, Rosalia Szettele, Helena Thoebert, Maria Andor, Maria Deutsch, holding Helen Deutsch Walker, and Eva Zettl, holding Eva Zettl Anile.

"As field workers, we got a little extra bread."
Maria Andor

Four days after her 16th birthday, Maria stands with the other townspeople who have been called to the town square. She has been evicted from her home, which has been looted of its possessions, and she now lives with several other families in another house. Gone are the feather quilts and the sturdy handmade beds. Like the animals in the barn she once liked to play with, she is expected to sleep on the straw-covered floor.

On this 28th day of December, 1944, the able-bodied women, aged 17-35, and the able-bodied men, aged 15-50, are gathered together. Wagons are loaded with sparse possessions, some food, and a few changes of clothing. The people are forced to walk 15 kilometers to Sombor, the county seat, where they are placed in deportation centers to wait for the trains. Weeks later when the trains finally arrive, they are herded aboard the cattle cars and forced to endure a three-week journey to Stalino, Russia, and years of unforgiving labor in the coal mines and rock quarries, many to die there of disease and malnutrition. Maria watches the children running about, and the women crying as the wagons begin to move.

Just under the age cutoff, Maria stays in Kruschiwl and is assigned as a worker to the partisans. She is taken as slave labor to different tasks every day. She never knows where she will be taken. She washes planes once in the airport at Sombor. She works in the fields in several neighboring towns a lot, on farmland, sometimes hers, that has been taken over by the partisans. Sometimes she works as a maid to the families of the Serbian colonists who are given the townspeople's homes. One family wants her to marry one of their sons—an offer she refuses. Her best job, by far, is baking bread for the partisans. There is always a little something extra to eat for the cooks and the bakers, and an opportunity to smuggle food to family and friends.

At night, whenever and wherever she finishes working, she is herded into basements or old barns strewn with straw and forced to sleep side-by-side with several others. The smell of sour, unwashed bodies in close quarters fills her nostrils.

Frustration, fatigue, and fear surround her. Lice are constant companions. The lice bring typhus. Rats run over her legs at night.

Her friend Christine hated the rats most of all.

"At night some people would pick them up and throw them against the wall. And in the morning, the dead rats would be missing."

◆   ◆   ◆

Lying in the straw, her eyes open to the half-light of dawn she can see framed in the gray square of the room's window. The sounds of footsteps outside and other girls rustling awake beside her signal the start of another day.

She, and many other young, strong teenage girls and women, have been assigned as field workers. Every morning they awaken from the straw, smooth down their hair and skirts, and wander outside to relieve themselves. If they get up early enough, they will have some privacy before the guards arrive.

The guards like to be greeted as "*comrade.*" They line the girls up in twos and give each girl a piece of bread for breakfast. Most of the girls are happy to be field workers because they receive extra food rations. The alternatives are few, and lying in the straw weak from hunger and dying of typhus and scarlet fever is no alternative at all. But that is the fate of many of those too young or too old to work. The children itch from scurvy and bug bites, and most people suffer from chronic diarrhea.

At 16, she is glad to take her place in line. Glad to receive her allotment of bread. And especially glad to take up her hoe and begin singing the worker's songs that the partisans like so much. The guards are happy to be guarding these beautiful young Swabian women. They begin a singing contest with the girls in their rows. As they march, the row that sings louder gets extra bread and extra smiles from the partisan guard.

The line begins to move. Her voice begins to rise. Her stoic little heart lifts just a bit as they leave the camp and its sour smell of death and disease. And as they march and sing their way out of the camp, her sweet 16 heart literally soars. Even though she says good-bye each time to the mother who raised her and the sister she played with, she is glad to leave this sad place of death she once called home.

She looks out into the fields from the road on which she walks a).
dew of a spring morning, and with her sad hazel eyes follows the flight ⸺
flying free on the horizon.

◆   ◆   ◆

Hungary was only four kilometers to the north—four kilometers to free-
dom—and here they were, lying in filth, starving in the Voyvodina, while one of
the greatest harvests in the breadbasket of Europe lay rotting in the fields. The
Swabians, with their productive farms, made up only 4% of Yugoslavia's popu-
lation, but yet they managed to virtually feed the entire country with their wheat,
corn, barley, and produce. Now they lie starving in concentration camps, hated
by their communist captors, who viewed them as Nazis and "enemies of the peo-
ple." These peasant farmers were dispossessed of their farms and livelihoods and
expelled from their homelands, so their homes and rich farmlands could be given
to the new 'colonists' from Bosnia and Montenegro, who had fought with Tito to
liberate Yugoslavia from Hitler and the Serbian king.

As they lie starving in the concentration camps, unable to coax the bounty from
the land they loved, for the first time in 200 years Tito had to turn to the world
for food relief. This country, which had once fed itself and much of eastern
Europe, had just bitten off the hand that had fed it.

But not all of their Serbian, Hungarian, or Croatian neighbors hated them. At
night, the brave with a will to live and stave off the terrible hunger would sneak
out of the camps and beg for food in the neighboring towns. Without the kindness
that these neighbors bestowed upon them in the form of bread and bacon fat they
could heat in the fire and dribble onto the bread—a treat they called 'Zigeuner
Speck' (gypsy bacon)—and the beans and old potatoes they scavenged from the
fields, many more Danube Swabians would have starved. These proud, self-suffi-
cient farmers, whose hard work had always blessed them with a bountiful har-
vest, were now forced to beg from neighbors to whom they had once sold food.

A smiling Katharina Burlem.

"When you are a teenager, you feel invincible. I felt very confident, very fearless. My mother worked for the partisans, and I felt like nothing bad would happen to me."

Katharina Thoebert Burlem

The Taste of Gun Metal

The teens in the camp meet one day near the town square for a get-together. They talk and laugh, a strange sight in this barbed-wire town that is now home to hushed conversations and fear. It feels good like this sometimes to forget. To talk, to laugh, to punch, to cajole. Life may yet hold unbridled possibility, despite this present place of uncertainty and death.

The partisan guard nearby does not like the sound of their laughter. He is annoyed by the lightheartedness he sees in the teens. They are suspect, these children of the Germans; they are surely up to no good. They must be taught a lesson.

He marches over, pulling his gun roughly from the waistband of his pants, and points it angrily at the shocked teens.

"What's so funny? You want something to laugh about?"

He looks at each one in turn, wide eyes staring back, and tries again.

"Are you making plans to escape? Eh? You can't fool me. You can just forget about that. You will never be able to run away."

A tall, young, pretty blond girl takes his bait.

"Run away. Run away? And where would we go?" The teens join her in nervous laughter.

In a quick, altogether too-fast move, he strides forcefully toward her and pulls her blond head to his chest and roughly sticks the gun into her mouth. The metal shaft scrapes roughly against her perfect, white, 14-year-old teeth, and her blue eyes open wide in surprise. The taste of gun metal oozes into her mouth. It is gray and gritty, but not like the cold steel feel she expects. The gun is hard as it probes the inside of her mouth, but it feels warm and smells like the man holding her to his chest.

He looks about at the staring teens, and pushes the gun back deeper into the base of her throat until she gags and the others stand transfixed in horror. It is strangely quiet, the sound of laughter sucked out of the air. Now only the lone cries of the geese sound overhead.

"How does that feel? Eh?" he growls. "Not so funny anymore, is it?"

He glances angrily at his audience.

"I could shoot you all right now. How dare you mock me? You will not run away from me—any of you."

He looks back at the blond girl held tightly against him. It is deadly still for several tortuous seconds. No one moves in this slow motion of terror. Suddenly, the light in the girl's blue eyes changes. A shadow drops like a curtain and the terror and surprise vanish. Her lips curl grotesquely over the barrel of the gun. What is that? Is she smiling or crying? What a strange look he sees in her eyes. Quickly, she jerks her head to the side, pulling the barrel of the gun out of her mouth. She coughs and spits it away and turns up into his startled eyes.

"Where would we go?" she repeats hoarsely. "Where would we run?"

She laughs again, realizing the absurd impossibility of the situation. Her laughter breaks the spell and a few of the others begin again to titter.

Again, he points the gun at them threateningly.

"Stop laughing or I'll shoot you all right here."

"You're not going to do anything," she says, full of a fearless adrenaline now.

Her mother works for the partisans. Her mother cooks for them and if she wanted to, she could tell on him—no worse—her mother could poison them. She could poison their food and kill them all. Why doesn't she?

"You're not going to do anything," she repeats, believing in her fearless heart that she will be protected.

It is frustrating for the guard to wield his gun at these teenagers and yet feel so powerless. It begins to drop in his hand, and he waves it dismissively at them, shoving it angrily back into the waistband of his pants, as he stalks dejectedly away.

Alone again, the teenagers stand quietly. Surprised eyes look at each other in newfound awe. When the guard is out of earshot, the tall, blond, 14-year-old beauty, who will one day grow up to be my aunt, smirks, throws her head back, and leads them all in laughing even louder than before.

◆   ◆   ◆

Like the Jews, with whom they share the horrible camp and refugee existence, the Danube Swabians make a chicken soup that is balm to their souls. Rich, salty, yellow broth, with limpid circles of fat floating on the surface. Pieces of turnips, carrots, and boiled chicken pieces swim about with noodles and start the Sunday meal. The chicken soup is a weekend ritual. Aunt Kathy, the beautician with the beautiful blond French twist, is the only one at the table who eats her soup the proper way. In a row of bowls tilting inward and spoons hungrily slurping up, Aunt Kathy's bowl is the only one that tilts away from the grain, bowl and spoon luxuriously arcing out.

On work days she is immaculately dressed in the pressed polyester smock of the beautician. Hair always perfectly coifed, the beautifully manicured frosty pink nails of her left hand delicately cradle a piece of toast while her right hand spreads on a perfect layer of Land O'Lakes unsalted whipped butter.

At 30 years of age, she starts another day as the entrepreneur she already is. Having saved money from working in factories since arriving in Chicago twelve years earlier, and sharing small one-bedroom apartments with her parents and sister, she is already the proud owner of Kathy's Beauty Salon on fashionable Sheridan Road. Aunt Kathy keeps her business for three years, until she moves to Hawaii to marry Ernie, a United States Marine she meets one year while on vacation.

Katharina, my mother's sister, was only 12 years old when the partisans occupied Kruschiwl. While my mother was away working in the fields from spring through fall, my aunt stayed with her mother in the camp. Because she was tall for her age, she was responsible for tending a vegetable garden. Her mother was able to look after her and see her often during the day, as she was responsible for cooking for the partisans, and the vegetable garden was directly behind the mess hall's kitchen.

Like many of the camp inhabitants, Kathy became very ill with typhoid fever, most likely contracted during the typhus epidemic which spread through the camp in the fall of 1945. Highly contagious, typhoid fever is spread by lice, which were a constant problem in the camps. People were rarely allowed to wash, and there was no soap or disinfectant. An occasional dip in the river would be the extent of hygiene during those years. The filth, plus the poor diet, made many people prone to illness. Many died of malnutrition, starvation, diarrhea, and disease.

Terribly ill, Kathy was unable to eat for three weeks. She became very weak, and lost all of her hair and the ability to walk by herself. She came very close to death, but at the worst point in the fever's cycle, her health turned miraculously for the better. She lived, but her illness killed something else inside of her. It destroyed her ability to ever conceive children. Being so young and at the crux of puberty when she became ill, the typhoid impaired her uterus from maturing properly. Years later, in an effort to conceive, she would stare tearfully with pain at a fluorescent light fixture overhead as doctors tried to blow up her uterus to make it a more hospitable place for a fetus to live. After years of fruitless fertility treatments and the adoption of two children, she finally conceived, but would be unable to carry the child to term. In the fifth month, the little boy, Stephen, was miscarried.

How she loved children, my Aunt Kathy. See her at 15 years of age in the refugee camps in Austria baby-sitting the children of the wealthy Austrians who lived nearby. And, then, as an immigrant in Chicago, her own love affair with me and my brother began. Giggling, blue eyes sparkling, head bent over my baby brother, Henry, she gently rubs his ribs with her beautiful hands.

"Talk to me," she says laughing. "Come on. I know you want to talk to me."

She tickles and goads him mercilessly. He laughs and squirms under her touch, but does not reward her with one syllable. A 2-1/2-year-old girl with crooked pixie bangs observes the scene carefully, and looks up to inform her aunt of what seems fairly obvious.

"He can't talk. He doesn't have any teeth."

Aunt Kathy laughs harder now with renewed glee.

"That's right," she repeats. "He doesn't have any teeth!"

My Aunt Kathy loves to laugh. Laughing is something she will never lose or allow anyone to take away from her.

◆   ◆   ◆

"How old are you?"

Children always ask the most direct, tactless, amusing questions. In the early 60's, and in some circles it still holds true today, you do not ask women their age. It's considered impolite. Five-year-olds are too young to learn all the nuances of tact, and I was no different. I was as merciless as they come with my who-what-when-where-why questions, too.

"How old are you, Aunt Kathy?"

"Twenty-five," she'd reply directly.

And the next year on her birthday I'd ask again and get the identical response. I was almost through grade school before I realized that my dear, lovely, laughing Aunt Kathy was still 25 years old. As far as I'm concerned, she always will be.

Maria Andor and Christine Kiefer, 2007.

"Wenn mir durch Gakowa geht und net ausgelacht wird,
Durch Kruschiwl geht und kein Schlee griegt,
Und durch Stanicitz geht und net angeschmirt wird,
Dann kenn mir durch die ganze Welt gehen."

(An old Danube Swabian saying)

June 27, 1997—Enroute to German Fest

It is a humid morning, the air so heavy and wet it presses against me like the damp towel Mother used to wrap me tightly in when I was a child with the flu. 'We need to sweat out the fever,' I remember her telling me. The feel of her hands was reassuring as she toweled me off after the hot bath and wrapped me tightly in blankets, smoothing the sheets neatly over my Vicks Vapo-rubbed, constricted chest.

Today she no longer hovers over me with concern; she sits beside me in her white Chrysler Concorde, the car she bought because of the big trunk. The trunk of the Chrysler is big enough for her lawn mower.

Can you see her? Sixty-eight years old, 5'2" inches tall, round and strong in the middle, dismantling the handles from the mower and lifting it into the trunk—handles to follow—so she can run off to the cemetery to mow her father's, mother's, and husband's graves? It's never good enough—what the groundskeepers do—she needs to do a touchup every now and then.

One time she drove all the way out to St. Joseph's Cemetery—it's way out west by Belmont and Narrangansett Avenues, next to the old Kiddieland where my brother and I went as very small children. She got all the way to the grave site, unloaded the lawn mower, reassembled the handles and rolled it up the hill to the headstone and then—nothing. I can see her standing there with the little drops of sweat forming on her upper lip, the pink flush to her honey-colored face, muttering "shiiiit, shiiit, shiiiit"—she says the 'i' in shit like 'e', yanking on the pull chord as if her life depended on it and—nothing happened. The damn mower would not turn over. But that doesn't stop her from going again to do her 'touch

41

up', only this time she finally gives in and goes with a new mulcher she bought on sale. Nothing stops my mother from doing whatever she puts in her head to do. Nothing and no one need dare.

We three are headed off to Milwaukee on this humid, close-knit morning for German Fest. I am driving my mother and her girlfriend Christine, who is in the back seat fretting about the weather. My mother, not to be outdone, chimes in.

"I don't know, Ingrid. It doesn't look so good up there."

The sky is dark and gray and I ride west on I-94, occasionally putting on the windshield wipers to clear away the intermittent showers. The girls are a little skittish, like newly harnessed ponies, hinting that maybe I should take them back home.

"Don't worry," I reassure them. "It will clear up when we get there. You'll see."

I have been looking forward to German Fest for a long time. One of the many ethnic summer fests the city of Milwaukee hosts on its magnificent, rambling lakefront festival grounds. German Fest holds the promise of good beer, good bratwurst, and good oom-pa-pa dancing bands. I'm even looking forward to the yodeler from Munich.

I have brought along my cassette recorder, consciously aware that I will have the girls captive with me in the air-conditioned car and not wanting to waste the opportunity to interview them more about Kruschiwl and the ordeal they suffered at the hands of the communists. But to get there, I take a circuitous route, through the stomach, where I always find a favorite, comforting subject.

Farmer's wives and daughters cook. They learn the ways of the kitchen and green growing things when they are very young. I can still hear the voice of my father extolling my mother's praises by telling me that she could cook a seven-course meal by the time she was 13 years old.

"I don't know about that, Henry," she'd say with her voice trailing off into an embarrassed laugh.

I could tell that she was charmed by his comment even though he was exaggerating a little. Unfortunately, to his dismay, I found the bedroom preferable to the kitchen then—reading romance novels by the armful took my attention away from peeling carrots and potatoes.

"Tell me about the food," I say.

"The food?"

"Ja, the food. Tell me, what is *echtes Donauschwaebisches Essen?*"

I want to know about their unique ethnic meals and how their cooking differs from the stereotypical, popular German food.

"Well, you know, our cooking is based on the Austria-Hungary ki

I have heard my mother start the food talk like this many times.

"It's a combination of styles, similar to Hungarian and Polish dishe:

I can see Christine's gray-tinged short bob begin to move in the rear view mirror. She pipes in from the back seat. This is a subject she also knows and loves well.

I get a list of meals with Wiener Schnitzel (breaded veal cutlet) and Sauerbraten (marinated pot roast) strangely missing. Cows were used mainly for milk, butter, and cheese, they explain. Unlike pigs, which were slaughtered by each family once a year, beef was available only through the butcher, and only on rare occasions. So, when they ate meat, it was primarily chicken and pork from their own livestock.

Chicken Paprikash—a Hungarian goulash heavily spiced with paprika to coat the chicken with a savory sauce—and Schweinebraten (pork roast) were common meals. After the pig was slaughtered in the fall, they also made sausages, ham, and bacon that would be smoked and left hanging from the barn rafters through the winter. It kept cool there. Whenever bacon was needed, someone would go out with the knife and slice off a piece for cooking, or for putting on a piece of bread for lunch, with a nice Hungarian pepper and a tomato on the side.

When I close my eyes and turn into an eight-year-old again, I can see my father and grandmother sitting at the kitchen table, a favorite pairing knife in their hands, cutting little bite-sized pieces of bacon and bread and eating it right off the knife blade. They never used forks for this meal.

"*Mir essen wie Bauern,*" they'd laugh and chew with delight.

That is how I learned that farmers can eat with knives alone.

One of my favorite memories of my grandmother is when I was almost 30 years old and she was telling me and my girlfriend, Linda, how they slaughtered the pig every fall.

"Die pig?" she asked. "You vant to know about die pig?"

And she'd look at us both with a twinkle in her blue eyes and begin to tell us about the yearly slaughter. It was a project that took an entire day for the men and women of the family to complete.

First, the women would get the cauldrons of hot water boiling to fill a large wooden tub. The tub is where the pig would be washed after being killed and de-haired, and prior to being butchered. Then the men would go about cornering the pig, which was not an easy task. They would have to get a good hold on the pig and stick the knife in the right artery before slicing the throat. My grandmother would look at us during this part of the story and put her hand up to her neck like a knife and make a slicing motion. Then they would hold the pig's head over a bucket to let the blood drain out. The blood would be used to make sausage and lunch meat. Once in a great while, after being poorly stuck, a pig would slip out of their hands and go running out into the street, leaving a bloody mess everywhere and an embarrassed family who could never live down the jokes.

Christine begins telling me about her specialty, *Sarma*. Sarma are cabbage rolls stuffed with meatballs. The girls are reminding me of the food of my childhood and I am starting to get hungry, thinking of all the delicious *Mehlspeiss* of my youth.

Being Catholics, they never ate meat on Wednesdays or Fridays, so they cooked a lot with flour. They made strudel to go with bean soup, *Pfankuchen* (pancakes) and *Palachinga* (crepes) filled with apples and cottage cheese, and *Schmarra*, little golden pancake nuggets I ate with canned peaches on Friday nights.

The mention of strudel is reminding me of my visits to Aunt and Uncle Becker. Tante Becker was my father's aunt. She and her husband sponsored my father and took care of him when he arrived in Chicago as an immigrant. They lived near Schurz High School on Chicago's northwest side, about a block and a half away from what later became my mom and dad's first apartment building at 3913 N. Kildare—a beautiful gray stone down the block from the old YMCA on Irving Park Road, my first home in 1956.

We used to go to see Tante Becker make strudel. What a project that was. Everybody would help—my mother, my grandmother, Uncle Becker. Everybody who liked to bake joined in our strudel party. We used Tante Becker's kitchen table, which she would clear and then fasten with a clean white sheet. I can remember looking up to see the skin on her arms flop as she pounded and rolled the dough on the flour-sprinkled table over and over again. Sprinkle. Pound. Roll. Sprinkle. Pound. Roll. Sometimes her arms would vibrate in her sleeveless house dress as she rapidly stirred the strudel filling.

She pounded and pushed and pulled that dough out until it was so thin you could see the sheet right through it. Her assistant bakers, poised at each edge of the table, would pull the dough carefully towards them, sometimes pulling too hard until a hole would appear and spread like a puddle in the thin membrane. Then they'd have to mend it, pushing the torn edges back together again.

Then came the part I loved best. Tante Becker would retrieve the bowl containing the strudel filling, and with a wooden spoon, begin flicking the filling all over the dough-spread table. Flick. Splat. Splot. Plop. Watery, raisin-studded cheesy blobs landed all over the table until the bowl was empty. Then, Tante would use the back of the wooden spoon to blend them all together. Tante's strudel helpers would join her in spreading the filling evenly over the dough. My nose conveniently reached the table then, my eyes were level with the raisins, and I alternated between smelling the sweet uncooked fresh dough and wondering what it looked like from above.

Tante Becker would then cut the dough in sections and roll it up into neat, thin, lumpy rolls. She gingerly placed them into silver loaf pans to bake. And, while they baked, the adults, happy and flushed, would wash their hands and return to the dining room to play cards and chat. Later, after the strudel had finished baking and cooling on Tante's sideboard, we would all sit and relish eating the warm strudel, fresh out of oven. The crust was so thin and delicate. I loved the apple strudel and the raisin and cheese strudel. The powdered sugar would leave a white mustache under my nose.

Christine has nimbly moved to the subject of *Flamkuchen* now, which is not a cake at all but a flat bread, like pizza bread or Pita bread, that they would eat with sour cream and paprika. Soon we are on the topic of cabbage and noodles. Christine made *Kraut Fleckeln,* too. Kraut Fleckeln are cabbage and tiny dough drops cooked in butter. They made noodles of all kinds, cooked with fat, with cheese, with poppy seeds, and even with a nutty flavored grain they got from the black reeds that grew in the fields. They grew peppers and cucumbers and tomatoes and onions and made delicious vinegary salads and creamy cucumber ones. From the fruit trees came marmalade of all kinds to sweeten the crepes and to use in the cookies and on the bread.

I am thinking of the *Zwetschen Knoedel* now, those yummy plum dumplings my mother makes when the plums are in season. She puts whole plums inside flour dumplings as big as a baseball, boils them, and then fries them a little in bread crumbs. They're really good with sugar sprinkled on them. I can eat two. I want one now. Chewy sweet dough and a tart purple plum inside. Afterwards, my plate is clean except for the two bare plum seeds off to the side.

Every so often a rain shower rouses us from our food orgy reminiscence and I hear the click of the mini cassette in the recorder, letting me know to turn the tape over. The talk of food has piqued their appetites and memories of home. I pass by Kenosha and Christine and my mother are telling me about the towns in Yugoslavia where they grew up. There were 86 strictly German towns and over 300 partially German towns strung like pearls along the Danube, extending north and east along the Hungarian and Romanian borders. They are laughing joyously now about the town saying they are trying to teach me.

"Say it slowly," I plead. "One more time. One more time."

r is enjoying herself now and once over the Wisconsin border, the
, begin to clear. Some lighter patches of blue peek out from the
sky. Christine pipes in to help her out with the town rhyme.

"Wܦ... mir durch Gakowa geht und net ausgelacht wird,
Durch Kruschiwl geht und kein Schlee griegt,
Und durch Stanicitz geht und net angeschmirt wird,
Dann kenn mir durch die ganze Welt gehen."

If we can get through Gakowa without being made fun of,
Through Kruschiwl without getting beat up,
And through Stanicitz without getting cheated,
Then we can make it through the whole wide world.

They said it carefully together, like school girls, my mother taking the lead like
she always does and Christine's voice joining in softly. They are laughing and
explaining to me why the towns earned their dubious reputations. I learn that
Gakowa is the bigger, prosperous town where people are a little uppity; Kruschiwl houses the anal retentive disciplinarians with the perfect little yards; and
Stanicitz is the town of the wheeler-dealer merchants—a place where country
bumpkins best beware on market day.

As I write this, I realize that the saying holds a special meaning for Christine
and my mother. They both made it out of Kruschiwl—I wish I could say without
getting beat up—and through the entire world before they ever actually got to
know each other on the northwest side of Chicago.

They met one day at the deli counter in the Butera Food Store on Elston Avenue. My mother was waiting her turn to get some cheap lunch meat when she
looked up and saw Christine wheeling her cart nearby. It was in the spring of
1980, just a few month's after my father's death. Christine was also a widow; her
husband had died of a brain tumor in 1977. My mother had heard about Christine from some friends at the German Club; she was a *landsleute*—people like us
from back home—and she lived down the block and around the corner on Ken-
nison Avenue in a neat Chicago brick bungalow. They exchanged greetings and
phone numbers, and became fast friends.

Christine cries out suddenly from the back seat of the Chrysler.

"Why didn't anyone know what was happening to us?"

I haven't the heart to tell her the truth.

They knew. The allies had been talking about expelling the ethnic Germans for a
long time, since the Yalta Conference, to keep peace in Europe and to further

divide up the land, and they couldn't stop the invading communists from jumping the gun, from rounding you up like farm animals to work and to die, shipping you off to Russia as gifts for their war reparations.

They knew. They put you in camps to prepare you for the official expulsions which weren't scheduled to begin until spring of 1945, according to the agreement reached at the Potsdam Conference. But, by then, the Russians had already helped themselves to your fathers and mothers as slave labor, and Tito's communist partisans had appropriated your homes, their possessions, and you. You were the vulnerable Germans, with the thinnest ties to Germany at the farthest reaches of the Reich, and you suffered the severest blows.

My thoughts drift to the plight of the Danube Swabians in Czechoslovakia and East Prussia, which was painfully reported by eyewitness survivors to Alfred M. de Zayas in his book, *A Terrible Revenge*. The Sudeten Germans in Czechoslovakia were interned in camps by the Czechs. They were forced to identify themselves as German by wearing patches on their clothing, which made them vulnerable to abuses by soldiers.

The Danube Swabians in East Prussia fared no better. It is they who perhaps suffered the worst of the Red Army's revenge over Hitler's *Lebensraum* policy and the savagery of the German-Soviet war. Had Germany been successful in Russia, Hitler would have continued with *Lebensraum*, a strategy in which millions of ethnic Germans were to be resettled into captured lands. In Poland, in 1939, Nazi soldiers murdered and drove out local villagers, burned their homes, and literally eradicated entire towns, plowing over any evidence that anyone had ever lived there.

Nemmersdorf, a village of Danube Swabians in nearby East Prussia, was invaded on October 20, 1944, only seven days before my mother's town was overtaken. As most men had been conscripted into the German Army, mostly women, children, and old people were killed. Any men found at home were beaten and executed. Women of all ages were raped repeatedly, and some were even found crucified, hanging naked from barn doors. Even infants were abducted from their carriages. This carnage was repeated in Methgethen in February of 1945 and in several other communities where the Red Army invaded.

Word of the Nemmersdorf incident did not spread as far as Kruschiwl, but it did spur a stream of approximately 500,000 refugees from East Prussia to flee across the Frisches Haff, the ice-covered bay separating the inner coastline from the Pillau peninsula on the Baltic. The refugees who did not perish when the weight of their own wagons broke the ice were forced to dodge low-flying Russian planes that bombed them.

Many refugees who braved their perilous treks in hopes of a sea rescue ultimately perished in the worst known sea disasters. On January 30, 1945, the Wilhelm Gustloff sailed from Pillau with 7,000 refugees and was torpedoed three times by the Soviet submarine S13. Only 838 persons survived. On April 16, 1945, a Soviet submarine L-3 torpedoed the Goya and claimed the lives of almost 7,000 refugees. Of a total of 6,000-7,000 refugees on board, only 183 persons survived. The popular and better-known sinking of the Titanic, in which 1,517 lives were lost, pales in comparison.

The sins of the father had come to haunt his sons.

The refugees were killed as they fled and they were going to be expelled anyway. Where were they to go? These were not Nazis, or brown shirts, or the screaming masses from Berlin. These were not Hitler's inner circle or his willing executioners. They were Volksdeutsche. Farmers. Nobodies.

The world didn't care, Christine. They had no sympathy for anyone or anything remotely German. They made no distinction between the Nazis and the Danube Swabians. You got caught in the cross hairs. While the world was rejoicing that the war was over and the Nuremberg trials were in process, you were suffering your own Allies-condoned revenge, war crimes of expulsion, in which innocent children, women, the elderly, and 13-year-old girls, like you, were put to suffer the world's retribution. You were being punished, and no one cared.

Instead I say, "You were Hitler's victims, too. You suffered the backlash, the harshest blow of all."

By now I have exited and am cruising through downtown Milwaukee looking for the festival signs that will lead us to the lakefront festival grounds. We get a great parking place at noon and join the small hardy group waiting for tickets. The air is heavy and humid with puddles here and there, but I have an umbrella and a program now and am noting all their favorite performers. I will keep them dry and entertained. Myron Floren is here with his lederhosen and his accordion, and I am determined to find that yodeler from Munich. But first things first. It's time to find a nice goulash or a bratwurst. It's been a long ride and by my watch it's lunch time right on the dot.

I get a beer and join the girls on the long table-clothed picnic tables that are jamming the food courts. I pick at my goulash; it's meaty, but not spicy enough for my taste. I console myself, knowing I can pick up a bratwurst later. Mom and Christine fare better with the Schweinebratten and my leftover goulash.

After we eat, we go to the stage where Myron Floren is playing. Myron Floren is the famous accordionist from the Lawrence Welk show who charmed everyone here with his playing every Sunday night. There are crowds of people here, mostly in the 55-80-year-old age group, their white caps shimmering in the distance. As we mill about, looking around for familiar faces, I spot Adam's smiling face, nodding in appreciation, at the foot of the stage. We exchange warm greetings and I watch his face, rapt with attention, turn and smile softly at the stage.

Adam, my mother's cousin, plays a mean accordion himself. He learned to play in Austria, a place where music has always been appreciated. For Adam, Austria was a place where a young refugee's heart could suddenly soar free. Like Myron Floren, he loves to play waltzes and polkas. Looking at Adam enjoying the music makes me remember seeing him holding his own accordion lovingly in his arms, with the straps anchoring it across his chest, his hands opening and closing it while a happy smile, like the one he wears today, creased his broad face.

He was not a grandstander; he just loved to play. Throughout the years, at family parties over the holidays, I remember him cajoling his only daughter to play with him.

"*Komm* on, Kathi, *Komm*," he begged her.

She'd squirm a bit, like all children with performance anxiety, but she always gave in to him, hauling out her child-sized accordion and letting him help her adjust the straps over her pretty party dress.

"*Eins. Zwei. Drei.*"

He'd tap his foot three times, give her a knowing look, and they'd start in together on the Lichtensteiner Polka. As Kathi got older, her reluctance only increased until she finally switched from the accordion to an electric guitar.

Adam looks at me and says with great sincerity, "I would give anything to play a duet with Myron Floren."

Christine is happy to see Adam because Adam's presence virtually ensures a good time. If Adam is around, there will be dancing. My mother's presence ensures there will be dancing, too, and I, the apple, have not fallen far from the tree. People around us begin to tap their toes and sing along, and couples start dancing at the foot of the stage.

"What do you say, Mom," I ask, "how about a polka?"

We move to the front of the crowds and begin dancing under Myron's knobby knees, and I can see his wrinkled elbows pushing his accordion open and closed. My mother has her dancing look on, the one where she puts that fixed

:r face and keeps her eyes moving from left to right. She's surveying
'or twirling room and to see if anyone's looking at her and smiling at
everyone and no one just to be safe. She leads me through the dancers without
really looking at me, her gaze fixed at least three feet beyond my shoulders at all
times. She loves to spin me around in rapid succession. I've learned to keep my
eyes fixed on the horizon. We dance at least four or five dances, and afterwards
when she's resting, I go back up with my camera to get some pictures of Myron
talking with his band on the Miller Stage. After the pictures are developed, I will
be at big hit with everybody, bringing them all copies of our special day.

We drift away from Adam, and Christine, my mother, and I spend the day
walking back and forth, from one end of the festival grounds to the other. We
watch the yodeler's act, the Austrian wood wind band, the parade of ethnic German descendants, and the Milwaukee Donauschwaben Club members, who per-
form a series of ethnic dances. First come the children, then the teens, and finally
the adults. The men wear black pants and vests, and the women are in dark-col-
ored dirndls, their faces flushed in the close heat of this post-thunderstorm afternoon.

The weather stays very hot and humid, but we refuse to buckle under it.
Around 4 p.m. we go all the way back to the stage near the entrance gate to catch
the musical stylings of Die Sterne der Heimat (The Hometown Stars). And, lo
and behold, who is sitting under the stage's sweltering tent, where nary a fresh
breeze has a chance to blow, but Adam, Sali, and their entourage. This time it's
my turn to dance with Adam. And, the band is playing my song, the Schnee
Waltzer (Snow Waltz).

Adam takes me by the hand in his very courtly manner and lets me precede
him to the stage. I turn to look at him in this 90+ degree heat and he looks posi-
tively cool. At 5'8" inches, with a progressively balding sandy gray pate, soft blue
eyes and full lips, he looks very comfortable in this milieu. The dance floor is definitely home to Adam. He finds his beat, pulls me to him, and with his arms and
legs he guides me on a magical ride.

Adam is a fantastic dancer. A smooth rhythm runs through his legs, and he
can glide you across the floor like a dream to the Schnee Waltzer.

> *"Schnee. Schnee. Schnee. Schnee.*
> *Waltzer tantzen wir.*
> *Ich mit dir. Du mit mir."*

The Schnee Waltzer is my favorite waltz. While we dance, I close my eyes and
imagine myself at the court of Maria Theresia. Everyone is dressed in their best

finery. The curtains on the paladin windows of the palace ballroom have been pulled back to reveal the snow falling outside. But none of the dancers notice. They move in perfectly coordinated circles, spinning in unison while the snow flies unnoticed outside. Horse-driven carriages wait patiently far into the star-filled night as the dancers waltz the night away.

That is how Adam can dance. My father had that talent, too. Back straight, he guided you with the power of his legs and the pressure of his hand against the small of your back. No upper body movement at all. Very dignified. When they were young boys, they learned to dance at the weekend dances at the *Wirtshaus* (the town inn and dance hall). Adam in Kruschiwl in the Yugoslavian Batschka and my father in the Romanian Banat. Dances were the main form of entertainment and social activity for the young Danube Swabians. With every move observed and commented upon by their elders, they were encouraged to perfect their dancing from early on in their youth. Many of the Danube Swabian men and women are very good dancers.

I watch the dancers spin about me, their heads and torsos slightly out of focus. Giddy, I start to laugh as we glide in our rhythm together, moving in step, spinning strongly in our little circle. He smiles and is pleased that I can follow him. We dance to five or six songs, and I am amazed that in this humidity this 74-year-old man is breathing easily and barely working up a sweat. After the sixth dance, we finally take a break, and he pulls a handkerchief from his back pocket and wipes his brow with a smile.

"You're a good dancer, Ingrid. Really. A good dancer."

I kiss him on the cheek, and as we leave the dance floor, I can see Christine's hopeful eyes upon him.

Christine Kiefer as a child (center) surrounded by her father and mother
and other family members.

*"Once I was sitting at a riverbank (in Germany) crying, and
a woman stopped and asked me why I was so upset.
I told her I was hungry, and for once, I just wanted to eat
until my stomach was full and I was satisfied."*
Christine Kiefer

June 10, 1998

I am at my mother's house, in my old bedroom that is no longer my bedroom, devoid of its pink walls and white Formica-topped girly furniture. I lie on my back and look out at pale yellow splotches of walls, struggling to peek through the crowded facade of a heavy, brown Mediterranean bedroom set that is much too large for this once spacious room. Where did this furniture come from, I wonder? Was it once in Oma's apartment, and my mother too loathe to give it up or sell it off has crowded it in here?

The basement, too, is filled with an odd assortment of mismatched furniture—orange vinyl and putrid green couches, chairs and end tables from the 60's, and mattresses converted into a funky queen-sized daybed that rests on the wall adjacent to the bar. Whatever was she thinking when she decorated that space? I suspect there was simply wall room there, as none of the other groupings make any more sense.

When I go downstairs in search of soda cans or ancient wine bottles filled with gritty sediment, I am struck by the oddity of the scene. Like an eclectic group of strangers invited to a party, the furniture mills about haphazardly in a polite, yet uncomfortable, way. Their only connection to each other is from her or his workplace, or from her or his crazy family. There is an undeniable emptiness in the midst of this clutter that is my mother's finished basement—just as there is in this room that was once mine.

I'm lying on my back on the side closest to the door on a twin bed that has been pushed together with another one to form a super-sized king. This king, I realize, now contains the two twins that once stood three feet apart, the beds my brother and I slept in for many years before it was deemed appropriate that he be moved into the bedroom off the kitchen and I be given my own pink and white room.

I'm lying on this enormous bed which now can hold all the grandchildren—all four of my brother's beautiful toddlers—when they stay for overnighters. They range in age from three to eight years old. No one is using this monstrosity now as a trampoline as I often do when those toe-headed urchins move my childish spirit to soar. Instead I lie here with an adult's sensibilities, vigilant to distant changing sounds of brisk-lipped, authoritative talk show hosts which blend later into the soft, melodramatic tones of daytime soap opera stars. Over the television in my mother's room, every so often I hear the sounds of a painful moaning and thrashing and the bereft sound of my own name called out of the din.

I jump up from my early morning reverie and go to her.

"My belly. My back. It hurts so much," my mother sorrowfully tells me. "Bring me some apricots and an English muffin. I'm so dizzy I can't even get up."

"I'll make you a nice fruit salad today."

I fly into the kitchen, my eyes barely open, grabbing a banana and a peach in one hand and opening the refrigerator for the muffins with the other. I pop a muffin into the toaster and begin to slice up a fruit salad so my mother will have something nutritious in her stomach so she can take her pain pills and get up to go to the bathroom.

I serve her in courses because it's easier to carry everything that way. I take the fruit salad to her first and then turn back for the muffin before sitting down at her side. She eats her fruit salad and muffin lying down. It is strange to see this fiercely independent creature squirming helplessly on her back. Stranger still to help her undress after breakfast, slipping off her pajama bottoms with her panties inside while she mutters at the same time for me to leave and give her some privacy. A fresh nightgown is slipped over her head and her face registers a grimace as she lies back and rolls slowly from side to side, pulling at either side of the nightgown.

"I don't know how this could have happened," she moans, as her head finally comes to rest on the pillow. "I have never hurt myself like this before. I feel like I'm on my last legs. Would you make me an egg for his other half of the muffin?"

"How do you want your egg? Scrambled? Over-medium? Po—"

"You can poach it."

I turn back into the kitchen and get to work. Over the last couple of days I have watched over her with a strange sense of detachment. How could this be, indeed? How could this mighty oak be felled? For four years when she was a prisoner of the partisans in the concentration camps of Yugoslavia she worked bent over, hoe to the tough ground, digging into the clay-baked earth. From field to field, town to town, bending, stooping, carrying, raking, harvesting, and hungering. But that was 50 years ago—she was still a teenager then—and that old thorn is nothing in comparison to this pain in her lower back she suffered from moving the living room furniture in some spirited, yet late, spring cleaning.

◆   ◆   ◆

Later in the afternoon my mother's girlfriend Christine comes for a visit and asks my mother if she still has her wurst. *Oh, yes.* She pulls up the front of her nightgown with the innocence of a third-grader and shows us the sausage-like swelling from her pulled stomach muscle. Apparently, pain from a back injury can circle around your middle, pulling muscles into painful knots of resistance. What else could explain this swelling unless she's developed a hernia or a very bad case of constipation? After a few minutes discussing these options, Christine and I leave her to rest and we visit awhile in the living room.

"How's the book going?"

Everyone asks you that when they find out you're writing one, and it's the hardest question to answer when you're not writing much.

"OK" is what I always say. "It starts and stops."

Christine doesn't want to cajole, encourage, or judge. She gifts me instead with a sudden urge to talk about her mother. Like an artist picking up a paintbrush, Christine begins to paint a heartbreaking scene. Between the lines of her simple, heavily accented speech, a picture unfolds from the gray undercoating of memory that holds me transfixed in the paradox of its simplicity and enormity.

At the center of the painting, a once robust woman lies limply in her husband's arms. He looks down into her ravaged face, lovingly caressing the damp strands of hair from her forehead. A young girl of 13, still innocent yet on the vulnerable edge of womanhood, stands in the foreground, hovering in the doorway. Her wounded gray-blue eyes, like the feathers of a dove, open wide in alarm at the scene unfolding before her. An old woman, clad in a heavy black skirt and kerchief, sits on a side chair; the pale light from a bedside table illuminates the downward cast of her nose and her gnarled hands which finger the beads of a rosary. Not sure if she should stay or run away, Christine stands helplessly, one hand on the doorknob and the other clutching her startled mouth.

She had just learned how to walk again after spending her 12th year recovering from a terrible bout with rheumatic fever. Soon her fingers would turn on the knob and she would have to walk without her mother to the other side of the door. There on the threshold she would behold yet another tragic scene. Christine continues her tale of how war can tear a family away from a girl and make her coming of age the most horribly defining time of her life.

It began sometime in 1943 or early 1944. The Hungarian army, which had jurisdiction over the ethnic German towns in the Batschka, drafted all the *schlossers* (locksmiths) in her home town of Kernei. Christine's father, Adam, was a schlosser and adept at metal works of all kinds, and he was called to work in an airplane factory in Budapest. The airplane factory was bombed constantly, and each day fewer and fewer men reported to work. The missing men were presumed dead. Adam wanted desperately to return to his home and family, so he took the opportunity of leaving one night, knowing in the morning he would not be missed.

He returned home safely to a joyous welcome and spent the next few months as normally as possible for young man AWOL during wartime who had to hide himself. He spent his fugitive days in the back of the house and in the courtyard where prying eyes could not see him and report his whereabouts to the authorities.

He had a large industrial grinder in the house that took up two rooms. The motor was in one room and the conveyor took up another. Prior to being drafted, he ground corn into meal for his neighbors so they could feed their livestock. During his time in hiding, the grinder was mostly still and he moved about quietly, he and his wife Elizabeth speaking in close whispers when they passed each other going back and forth from the house to the barn. Life went on quietly until October 20th arrived. That was the day the Russians invaded and parked a tank in the backyard.

"Die (the Russians) took all the men and women up to age 35 to Russia to work in the labor camps," says Christine." My mother, who was 36, was taken from us on Christmas Eve to work in a hospital in Sombor. She was supposed to take care of the wounded soldiers. My father's mother who lived with us and I visited her once. But, at that visit, she told me not to come back. She wanted me to hide myself in a babushka and be careful to stay out of sight of the soldiers. She was afraid they might rape me. From then on my grandmother took my nine-year-old sister, Gertrude, to visit."

"What did your father do after your mother was taken?" I ask.

"He went around to other mills in town to help out the townspeople. The mills had been abandoned by people who left for Germany before the Russians came. Die (the families) had men who were soldiers in the German Army and Die had to leave. Even though my father wasn't in the German Army, he wanted to go then, too. But my mother wasn't ready. She didn't want to leave her stuff."

Christine's eyes look away for a moment into the empty space of a lost opportunity.

"The next time I saw my mother, she was being carried into our house by my uncle. He laid her on the bed. We had gotten word from the hospital in Sombor that she was suffering from a fatal illness and would be released to come home. I don't know exactly what she was sick from but it could have been typhus; so many people died of that then."

"My uncle hitched a wagon and my grandmother went with him to pick her up. My father, who was still hiding, had to stay behind and wait. When they brought her in, my father went to her and stayed at her side all that night and the next day."

"She died in his arms the next night. I don't remember what was said. I don't think my mother could talk. I don't think she was conscious. All of a sudden we were all crying. My father, my grandmother, and I were all crying, and that is how I knew she was gone."

In the midst of my mother's vulnerability pressing in around me, tears spring to my eyes with this vision of a frail, dying woman languishing in her husband's arms and their 13-year-old daughter hovering in the foreground. The thought of Christine losing her mother this way is more than I can bear and I jump quickly to my feet, go to her, and bend my cheek to hers in a quick hug. She's flushed and misty-eyed.

"You poor baby," I murmur and hug her firmly, holding her to me like a precious child, the tears of the present and the past mingling together on our cheeks.

◆   ◆   ◆

June 25, 1998

This need to know more and not wanting to all at the same time is the hardest, push-me, pull-me thing about writing this book. But I stumble on and find myself sitting in Christine's TV room in the back of her house, sharing an ice coffee on an unseasonably warm and humid day in Chicago.

The rest of the house is all closed up and immaculately sweltering. The ivory chintz curtains in the living room hang low over natural wooden sills that were once hand-varnished by Christine. It was such a long time ago, but they look brand new and crisp, the natural patina of the wood shining through. The sills, flat, smooth, and shiny, show not even a whisper of gray-beaded dust—not even in the corners where they meet the edge of the window.

We sit in the enclosed back porch of her bungalow where it is cool and the clinking of ice cubes and the droning of the window air conditioner makes us feel safe and secure enough to talk of our mothers and death and dying and other hardships that 13-year-old girls should not have to bear.

"What happened after your mother died?" I ask and raise the glass to my lips.

The coffee is cool and sweet and creamy, with a hint of sharpness that is later revealed to me as Kahlua, while I linger on Christine's front steps preparing to go and wondering why I feel slightly befuddled.

"I don't remember if a priest was there. We got a plain wooden casket without flowers or anything and just took her in a wagon to the cemetery and buried her."

"What did your father do after your mother died?"

"After a couple of months while we were mourning the death of my mother, Die (the Russians) left and the partisans came. Die (the partisans) forced my father to do things he didn't want to do. Die (the partisans) looted all the homes and Die made my father move everyone's furniture out of their houses. He had to put everything out on the street, and a wagon came to pick it up later."

Christine's eyes look down in embarrassment over her father's powerlessness. I can imagine how difficult it must have been for him to knock on all of those doors, standing before his neighbors with his eyes to his toes and his hat in his hand.

"Things got worse. By springtime, Die (the partisans) took us from my father. On Good Friday, Die made me and my grandmother walk my grandfather 13 kilometers to Kruschiwl to the concentration camp Die built in your mother's town. My grandfather had had a stroke and he was numb on one side of his body. The three of us limped along, with him in between us, wearing nothing but knitted slippers the whole way."

Can you imagine that, her sputter says, in a way that recalls the futility of the incident.

"Not long after, maybe a month or two later, my grandfather died in the camp. We sewed his body into a blanket and Die loaded him on a wagon with other dead bodies. He was buried in an unmarked mass grave on the outskirts of town."

"In the camp, I, my grandmother, and my sister, Gertrude, struggl
alive. We never had enough food there, so I had to sneak out at night ar
ging. We went begging at the *bustas*, the farms of Serbian and Hungarian townspeople who were left alone by the partisans. Sometimes they had something to
spare—some bread, beans, or yellowed, rancid bacon—that I could take back to
the camp and share with the others. The mothers used to beg for the children in
the camps, but I had no mother anymore, so I had to do it."

"We used to walk like this."

Christine gets up momentarily to show me how she shuffled along with the
other beggars in an orderly line, each one taking their turn, mouths pleading sorrowfully *bitte* (please) and hands outstretched. She sits down to laugh in an
embarrassed, tired way that sounds like she's about to cry.

"One time when I was begging, I was walking near a dried out ravine. I was so
tired I fell asleep on my feet and stumbled into the ravine."

A lone tear leaks out of Christine's right eye and sits precariously on her bottom lid. We sit speechless for a moment and I take another sip from my glass.

"How did you get out of the camp in Kruschiwl and get to the one in
Gakowa?"

"One day my father sent a messenger to the camp in Kruschiwl asking us to
leave the camp and meet up with him. So one night, my grandmother, sister, and
I escaped and we went back to Kernei to my father. He hid us in one of the abandoned mills he was working in. It was much better there; my father brought us
food."

"How long were you there before the partisans found you?"

"After about two months, Die found us out and, this time, Die sent my father
and me to a working camp in another town named Gakowa. There we were
assigned to work on the farms. We got a little more food on the farm because our
people cooked and it was like home-cooked meals. My grandmother and sister
had to go back to the camp in Kruschiwl."

"How long were you in Gakowa?"

"After a few months went by, my grandmother sent word that Die (the partisans) wanted to take my sister, Gertrude, away from her and put her into an
orphanage. So my father and I had to go back to Kruschiwl to stop it. Because he
was still alive, Gertrude was allowed to stay with us, and he decided to stay there,
too, so we could all be together at least."

"Not long after that we decided to escape together into Hungary, and from
there we went to Germany. In Germany, we weren't wanted either. Die (they)
sent us from one refugee shelter to another. I stayed in seven different camps, can

you imagine that? Thirty to forty people to a room, young children fighting at night—you couldn't sleep."

"Die (the Germans) didn't want us. There wasn't enough food there either; I understand. Once I was sitting at a riverbank crying and a woman asked me why I was so upset. I told her that I was hungry and for once I just wanted to eat until my stomach was full and I was satisfied."

"That is why I love to eat anything I want," she says with a grin and a twinkle in her gray-blue eyes. "And, I love sweets. If I ever get diabetes, I think that would just kill me."

◆   ◆   ◆

June 12, 1998

Three days after changing, bathing, feeding, and medicating Mom, microwaving wet towels for her back and filling sippie cups with a variety of beverages, I am finally allowed to go to my home where it is strangely quiet and empty. Thursday passes in an out-of-body haze in which I make checkup calls throughout the day. Friday thankfully brings me a new assignment. In the car on the way to the doctor, I make my proposal. I'm driving the big white Chrysler Concorde that is much too big for her and awkward to handle. I don't like the car. The brakes are too soft, and the car isn't nimble enough. I worry about her safety and mine.

"While you're recovering from your back injury," I begin, "you're not going to be able to do a lot of things at the building. While you still have this building and I'm out of work, I can help you. I'll be your assistant property manager. You tell me what to do and I'll do it. And you can pay me. We can help each other. What do you think about that?

I look over and notice how cute she looks in her matching brown stretch pants and gold-printed top.

"Right now I'm just concerned about this pain in my stomach and what it is and when it's going away."

Did I lose her on the 'you can pay me' part?

Letting go is a difficult process. Letting go of failed relationships, soulless jobs, a pain in the back, and most of all, an identity—a world of memory and work and independence and routine all wrapped up in a building that's both a joy and a curse. Believe me, I want to shout, I understand. But, like my mother, I know that now is not the time to tell her I've decided to sell my house and continue on in my chameleon self-studies. Quietly I take the Chrysler back to Evanston where just minutes ago I began the journey.

Back and forth and back again in time. Traveling along the same streets and byways of my youth. I spend so much time going sideways, I wonder how much progress I'm actually making. With this book. With this woman.

PART II
Deportation to Russia

For decades, Kruschiwl sat atop shifting sands of changing political allegiances. Prior to 1919, it was part of the Austria-Hungary empire. In 1919, after the First World War, it was parceled away and established as Yugoslavia for the first time. In 1941, after the fall of Belgrade to the Nazis, it was placed under the jurisdiction of Hungary. And, in 1944, as the Nazis began their retreat from Belgrade, Tito's partisans reclaimed it as Yugoslavia.

In the fall of 1944, the occupying partisans deported all able-bodied Danube Swabian men, aged 15-50, and women, aged 17-35, to Russia as slave labor to serve as reparations for the Soviet Union's participation in defeating the Nazis. Stalin was allowed to take Danube Swabians to help rebuild parts of Russia that were destroyed during the war.

Of the 874,000 Danube Swabians who were deported, 45% of those perished in Russia. A total of two million Danube Swabians died as a result of enslavement, flight, and expulsion.

Helena Deutsch in Kruschiwl.

Picture a table of Danube Swabian immigrants. It is Thanksgiving.

In the photographs, they are always grouped together around a table laden with goodies of all kinds. There are always three meats to choose from, usually turkey, ham, and a bowl of Hungarian sausage, spicy and juicy when your teeth bite down into that crisp, taut skin. There is always a hot vegetable, or two, or three. Usually the green beans have been *eingebrennt,* cooked with flour and lard and salt to coat them in a rich, tasty gravy. Mashed potatoes are plentiful, as well as the cold variety. Rosalia's (Sali's) potato salad is simply the best—creamy and rich with paprika-sprinkled hard-boiled eggs arranged perfectly in thinly sliced spheres over a rocky, teaming bowl of potatoes. My mother, Maria, makes the best cole slaw, with just a hint of sweetness and a nice blend of vinegar and mayonnaise. This is a hardy, tasty, chewy slaw with plenty of cabbage and carrots and green pepper and celery, with lots of restraint on the *schmear.*

And, there is bread. Let us not forget the bread. The staff of life. There is always bread on my mother's table. Usually some dinner rolls and a nice fresh loaf of white Italian bread and always some bakery sliced rye bread on the side. Before any meal, while the bowls of food are still being prepared for serving, there stands my apron-clad mother, eating a piece of bread while she works. It is usually the end piece, the hard crusty end piece that gets her full attention. This is the heel of the bread that demands respect and fortitude from the chewer, but it is child's play for bread enthusiasts like her who delight in its complex, rough texture. She has learned years before that eating an end piece gives her more—more chew, more texture, more satisfying eating time when you're hungry and there isn't much else to eat.

For dessert, there is always plenty of variety there, too. Homemade cookies of all kinds, made from recipes shared in families for hundreds of years. Apricot-filled sugar cookies, egg white and walnuts in crescent shapes, chocolate-layered, julienne sandwich wafers, bear paw sugar and nut cookies, and there is always a seed and an almond strudel. Aunt Sali and Grandma Thoebert always make the best *Kremschnitte* (creme slices). The phillo dough is always papery thin and delicately crisp with a generous sprinkling of powdered sugar.

These immigrants gather around the table in their photos, proudly showing off their largess—these tables laden with proof of their survival to the good life. See how well they eat. See how well they are all doing. The table overflows and they are together again—families once torn apart are joined together in a celebration of a holiday which commemorates their saga perfectly. Persecuted and despised for who they were, they were driven from their homelands to live quiet lives of desperation as refugees in foreign lands that did not welcome them, only to seek a better life in America and a table laid with the promise of a full belly, fully satisfied.

Thanksgiving is the best holiday of all for immigrants to celebrate.

In photos they also pose gathered together at weddings and summer events, the more the merrier. Grouped tightly together, like stitches in a quilt, they stand close beside each other, fitting in as many as they can gather in the picture. In perfect rows, like smiling kindergartners they pose, or in artful half-moons. They say, look how plentiful we are. Look at how we stick together. In thickness and in thin.

There is strength in this unity. See it in the hallways at the weddings. See it grouped squinty-eyed in the bright summer picnic light at Lake Villa. See them spinning together in perfect polka-step on the wooden dancer's stage. We are still in step. We are still together. We are still strong. We are still perfectly in control. We are immigrants. We are pioneers. We are survivors one and all.

Not bad for the war refugees. Vagabonds who once traveled by wagon and train, by boat and by foot, hated for who they were, begging for food, seeking comfort in refugee camps, the government homeless shelters for displaced people in Germany and Austria. There was not much there for the refugees in those lands either. The war had dissipated resources. Food levels were disappointingly low. And, for these penniless immigrants, who had been expelled from their homelands, there were not many places left to go. And they were not welcomed in stressed European nations—these eager, hungry, displaced Danube Swabians.

◆   ◆   ◆

Grandpa Thoebert

When he drank too much, which he invariably did—usually whiskey shots, beer, Rhine wine, and Seven-up spritzers—his mind would go back to the land he had lost. Whoever sat closest by him at the table—usually his brother-in-law, Jakob-vetter, or his cousin, Petervetter—would feel him lean in close, see the rosy flush in his cheeks, the dangerous sparkle in his light blue eyes, and smell the wine on his breath when he started in with his "Remember when...." Would there by any takers in this strange table game that played on loss—the loss of land and dignity? And soon enough the arguments would begin about the trivialities of the size of the fields or which direction the walkway along the old house went.

"The walkway went east and west," my Grandfather, Jacob, would assert.

"Na, na, Jacob," Petervetter would reply good-naturedly with his deep, soothing bass, "it went north and south."

"No, Petrich," my grandfather's voice would raise with irritation, "it went east and west.

"Na, na, Jacob, "Pettervetter's voice failing to soothe.

"Ja, ja, Petrich."

Grandpa Thoebert was lost again.

This type of conversation went on and on with some patient bass murmuring sounds coming from those beside him and the higher-pitched laughter of the women farther away, only to have him become even more incensed. The triviality of his insistence took on immeasurable importance because it represented the walkway in front or alongside the house that led into the place that once was his. His castle, his domain, his home that was taken and inhabited by Tito's cursed partisan soldiers.

He'd stand and bang at the table with his face flushed and his fist hard, angry at God and cursing Tito's name for forsaking him. Those around him, like Peter-vetter, who had better control of their emotions and the losses they had sustained—those who had learned to not despise him for his continuing weakness that recalled their own painful suffering—would look about the table with hooded eyes, slanted with disapproval, but with patience, too.

Sometimes my grandmother would laugh at him. Uncomfortable with his difficulties and these displays of emotion, she would make fun of his drunkenness and his inability to maintain his dignity and self-control in front of the others, who each in their own way carried the heavy baggage of the past.

◆   ◆   ◆

Look closely and you can see them carry their bundled up sheets filled with meager belongings. Walking for kilometers, like cattle being herded to concentration camps, bundles crowding together, clutched close and in. Bundle to bundle they stand, thousands of teeming frightened people, crowded together from towns around and about until they are encamped 20,000 strong in a town in which less than 1,000 people comfortably lived. Such was the fate of their town, Kruschiwl, which was turned into a massive concentration camp.

This macabre transformation of Kruschiwl into a concentration camp was repeated in Danube Swabian villages throughout the Batschka and the Banat, in peaceful villages like Rudolfsgnad, which had a Jewish Commandant who had survived the Nazi camps, and in the towns of Gakowa, Jarek, Mitrowitz, Molidorf, Kerndia, and Walpach. Perhaps even more macabre than the camps themselves is to learn that the person credited with their design, Moise Pijade, Tito's closest advisor, was a Jew. The white gothic letters of the camp names haunt me and burn out from black crosses while I pause at the memorial in the Lake Villa home of the German Aid Society. On a refuge of private land in Lake County, a far northern suburb of Chicago, a silent minority quietly mourn and remember their dead.

◆   ◆   ◆

Look closely and you can see the bundles falling in the wagons as the able-bodied are herded to the trains for Russia. Look closely and you can see the bundles bouncing erratically against their backs as they run at night through cornfields. The moon illuminates that lump as they crouch lower in the grass near the riverbank, waiting with the guard they had bribed for the boat that would come to take them across the border to safety. See how the boat drifts closer, in between the cruising Russian gun boats on the river.

◆   ◆   ◆

Peter and Maria

Petervetter and his wife, Maria, waited one night with their bundles at the river-bank. With fear making their whispers sound harsh and loud, they crouched low in the grass, hearts pounding as they waited.

Maria had been able to cleverly sew some money and the last of her jewelry into the hem of her skirt. The night before their escape, she sat carefully pulling the stitches to retrieve this ticket to freedom. Running through the woods with their bribed guard, she was gripped with fear that he might turn against them and morning would find them floating face down in the shallow water.

Instead, she remembers how it feels to lie flat in a boat, with her face pushed hard against the cold, damp hull. If she could only press down harder, she would. Peter lying beside her pulls his head up carefully like a cobra out of a snake charmer's basket and gazes across the softly rippling water. Seeing Russian patrol boats in the distance, he says a silent prayer of thanks as the boatman comes aground on the Austrian shore.

◆   ◆   ◆

Like all able-bodied men, aged 16 to 50, and all able-bodied women, aged 17 to 35, Peter and his daughter, Helen, were taken to Russia to work in the coal mines at Stalino. Loaded into cattle cars and told they would be on a three-week temporary work assignment, they began the journey in December of 1944 that would ultimately bring him to this place by the riverbank.

Helena was 16-1/2 years old then, just under the age cutoff imposed on the workers sent to Russia. She did not have to go, but she chose to accompany her father anyway. The Russians wanted as many Danube Swabians as they could get to rebuild Russia from Hitler's war destruction, and Helena was an obedient, devoted girl who could not bear parting from her father.

They began their journey by foot, walking nine kilometers south to the city of Sombor. In Sombor, they were placed on cattle cars, crowded together, sleeping while standing or sitting up. For three weeks they traveled like this to Russia with only the minimal food and water they brought along. At night, at gunpoint, they were allowed to leave the train for ten minutes to relieve themselves, and then find some clean snow to drink and use to wash their faces. Exhausted and weak, they finally arrived in Stalino three weeks later and were then force marched another 15 kilometers to the labor camp. Helena fell often in the deep snow and Peter helped her up and along as best as he could.

At the camp, work in the coal mines was brutally hard. The frigid Russian winter did not help. Tattered, insufficient clothing and meager food supplies were the order of the day. While Peter slaved in the coal mines, Helena was assigned to work in the sanitarium of a local hospital in Stalino. It was there in April of 1945, within a couple of short months after their arrival, that Helena became ill and died from typhoid fever and malnutrition.

Soon after Helena's death, Peter made plans to leave Russia and return to Maria in Kruschiwl. Using money and valuables he had been able to smuggle into the camp, he bribed Russian guards to release him on a transport back to Yugoslavia. In September he began his journey, traveling by train through the farmlands of Hungary. At night, when the train stopped, he jumped from the car to scavenge and beg for food from the people who lived in the surrounding countryside. When he finally arrived in Kruschiwl, he discovered that Maria had already fled the camp and was in Hungary. Peter eventually went to her there, and together they mourned with bitter tears, as only parents who lose children can, the death of their only child—and later, to crouch low in fear on a riverbank in Hungary, to begin anew the second leg of their escape to freedom in Austria.

◆   ◆   ◆

There they sit together at the Thanksgiving table, gray heads bent over, methodically savoring the spicy, familiar taste of a Hungarian sausage. Married for 70 years, they take their rightful place at the table, giving new meaning to the phrase, "through thickness and through thin."

Through trials and adversity, hunger and loss, the horrible experience of the death of his only child, Peter still enjoys spearing the wurst with liver-spotted hands and carefully slicing it into perfect bites. He eats patiently, methodically, thoroughly—not in the hurried way that some of them do who know the nagging pain of hunger, like a knife that scrapes you thin from the inside. Side-by-side, through bad times and through good, at my mother's table eating wurst, or drenched with fear and dampness, crouched low in the river grass, or with bodies pressed tightly together in the hull of an old rowboat. Side by side, they are bound together with this shared experience for all eternity.

I watch the thin wisps of his dark hair stick closely to his moving, balding pate and the rhythm of his thin cheeks like a steady breath go in and out, in and out, as he carefully swallows his wurst, placing his fork carefully at the edge of his plate and his hand gently on my grandfather's arm.

"Na, na, Jacob," he murmurs reassuringly, as if to say,

East or west? North or south? Na, na, Jacob. It really doesn't matter anymore."

Jacob and Helena Thoebert at their 50th wedding anniversary.

Saturday Night at Oma's in the 60's

My brother and I are scrambling to the top of the immaculate first floor landing of my grandmother's huge 13-flat apartment building. Clomp, clomp, clomp up the carpeted stairs with mommy and daddy close behind, anxious to begin their evening alone together. By the time we reach the first door on the right, 12 steps up exactly, it swings open wide to reveal Oma—our beautiful, strong, blond-haired, blue-eyed grandmother, framed in the doorjamb, holding out her arms and calling to us in delight.

"Meine Engelskinder," (my grandchildren) she calls out with glee. And my brother and I each get a turn being smothered to her breast and getting the repeating cheek kiss. First one loud smacker to the right. Then another to the left. Again to the right. Yet again to the left. After my brother Henry and I have been extravagantly smothered and smooched, I look up to see Oma beaming down at us with that undisguisable look of delight, pink color in her cheeks, a sparkle to those blue eyes.

Engelskind. As a word literally translated from the German, it means much more than grandchild. It means child of the angels. And that's exactly how I feel when I am with my Oma. Somehow I am elevated, larger than life, and infinitely more appreciated, extra-special—*super-cali-fragi-listic-expi-ali-docious*—just like Julie Andrews used to sing in Mary Poppins.

"Come. Eat something. What can I get you? Let's look in the kitchen."

It doesn't matter that we have just eaten dinner with our parents. Oma's refrigerator and pantry cupboards are always well-stocked for grandchildren, filled with pop, ice cream, cookies, crackers, and chips. Oma and I both like the almond-studded windmill cookies, crisp on the teeth with the taste of nutmeg and ginger on the tongue.

Later, even better fed, we sit on the pullout couch in the living room that will later convert to our bed, and watch Get Smart on television. Oma makes popcorn, and I watch the light from the TV flash out from the screen, illuminating the wide-open mouthed, snoring face of my grandfather, sitting in his easy chair off to the side, with his thick gray ceramic beer stein slipping out of his hand. With smooth, practiced movements, Oma puts the popcorn on the rectangular cocktail table before us and turns around to pull the stein out of his fingers and right it on the little lamp table beside him. She turns back to join us without even a backward glance.

I am sprawled lengthwise on the couch now, feeling the rough crocheted brocade from the pillow cover on the back of my neck. Oma sits on the opposite end of the couch, putting my feet in her lap.

"*Kitzel mich, Oma. Kitzel mich* (tickle me)," I say.

And like she does all the many times I ask, she removes my socks and begins to stroke the bottom of my feet. It tickles a little, in that delicious way that sends shivers to my head, circling my ears, but mostly, it feels very comforting. Oma's large, veiny hands are warm and soothing to the touch. I begin to drift away, my feet warm and cuddly and tickly in her lap, sleeping the sleep that only a child of the angels can.

◆   ◆   ◆

A Thursday Night at Mom's in 1997

I'm not supposed to write about the fact that my grandmother married my grandfather on the rebound and lived for 50 years in a loveless marriage. It's the kind of family secret you're not supposed to talk about, let alone publish in a family history. Be that as it may, it does make for some interesting copy.

◆   ◆   ◆

"Who told you that?"

My mother's hazel eyes zero right in on me, as she turns from her place at the stove and pulls out the kitchen chair next to me. Spooning in leftover vegetables into a never-ending array of plastic Cool Whip bowls has suddenly lost its allure, and with her strawberry blond head entering into my peripheral vision, I am keenly aware that I have captured her usually divided attention.

I am relating some of my interesting family findings to my brother, the FedEx pilot I see only four or five times a year. He and I are making adult talk at the dinner table, something I know he cherishes because the discussions he has with his children run along vastly different topics. All four of them, ages three to eight, are busy watching Disney videos in his old room off the kitchen, which Mother now uses as her sewing room and video arcade. His wife, Sharon, is sitting to his left and she is enjoying a salad. Sharon is the only person I know who eats her salad after the meal. Henry is my only brother, and he and I get together infrequently, usually here in the home where we grew up, usually at the kitchen or dining room table. Our infrequent meetings are not because he is a pilot and is out of town piloting, but because he lives in Wheaton, a very out-of-town place to me. But that is another story.

"Do you remember," I begin with my brother, Henry, "when we were young and mom and dad would drop us there for overnighters when they went out to weddings and stuff? Remember how he would get drunk and mad at God for everything that happened in Yugoslavia—everything they lost—and his stroke—and how he would start banging his fist on the table? Remember how Oma would out-and-out laugh at him and egg us on to laugh with her?"

He drank. She ridiculed him. *Or was it the other way around?*

"Look at him," she'd say incredulously, eyes wide and taunting, "just look at him," and I couldn't help but giggle watching the red rise in his face and the light blue in his eyes flash with anger.

"I remember him going into the pantry six or seven times a night, shooting down some Schnapps and then filling his stein with beer," says Henry.

No, they were not a happy couple, we readily agree.

My mother sits down and beams her hazel eyes at me on high.

"Who told you that?"

My mother's insistence has betrayed her. I know instantly by the way she asks the question that it is true.

Her mother was one unlucky lady in the love department. But it is not hard to figure out anyway. Just look at the pictures of them standing there side-by-side over the years, so oddly mismatched from the start. She, the tall, striking, blond-haired beauty with the blue eyes. He, the short balding fellow with the egg-shaped face and the altogether too-big nose.

There they stand beside the gaudy silver Christmas tree, the one with the revolving color wheel that casts harsh shadows across their faces. Holidays turn into birthdays. Birthdays turn into anniversaries. And there they still stand, painfully erect, chins jutting, never touching, never smiling with sheer unadulterated joy. No, they are always posing dutifully for the camera.

Yes, we're still together, they say with their straight backs. *Yes, we're still together,* they say with the firm stubborn edge to their mouths. But the eyes, the happiness is always absent from the eyes.

◆   ◆   ◆

In Kruschiwl, as in the other villages along the Danube where ethnic Germans made up only 4% of the country's total population of Serbians, Croatians, Bosnians and Hungarians, people strove to protect their fragile minority cultures. Children were raised and expected to marry within the fold, however slim the pickings might be. The young were watched closely as they came of age by the older women, the black-kerchiefed crows who came to watch them dance. Every weekend there was a dance at the hotel dance hall. There wasn't much else to do for fun but waltz and polka. And, any boy who had the slightest desire to get close to a young girl would learn how to dance. Many a young romance began on an old wooden dance floor.

On Saturday nights the crows flew in to form rings around the periphery of the dance floor. The old grandmothers, at their favorite perches, watched every move. Look at that one. Look at this one. See how well they move together. See how well they dance. He has a nice rhythm. She has a pretty smile. They seem to like each other, they say with their knowing looks, their black-hooded, nodding heads. We should encourage them. They would make a good match.

◆   ◆   ◆

The story, what little I know, goes like this. She wanted someone else, but he was intended for another. And, even though she got a lot of offers, she picked Ota because he had some celebrity status, having come to Kruschiwl with his parents from America, with a few dollars in his pocket and enough land to recommend him. She married him for security, not for love. And the man who got away? He was one of the unlucky ones that died in Russia.

"Who told you *that?*" my mother asks again, hazel eyes narrowing.

I know I have sparked a sudden concern in her for the skeletons I may stumble upon in the family closet. *How far will I go? How much will they tell me?*

I assume the Fifth (amendment).

"I have been talking to many family members about their experiences, and someone, never mind who, told me that about Oma. I can't tell you who because a journalist never reveals her sources."

She laughs out loud, hard like a bark, and I know it's OK. I can write about Oma's unhappy marriage if I want to, but it's a good thing that it's not the main objective of the book.

Peter Becker and Jacob Thoebert.

March, 1998

I want to know. And I don't want to know. But I keep asking anyway.

"How did it happen that some of the men joined the German army? Did recruiters come door to door?"

"We got letters."

"Did they have town meetings and rile people up?"

"Yes."

"Why did Ota go with the Germans?"

"I already told you."

My mother is getting impatient with me, like she always does when I need to keep asking to get more information from her, or when she is not sure of the right answer. I know from the feedback I've received from those who have seen my manuscript that people need to know how much choice there was for those caught in the middle of Hitler and Tito, fascism and communism. Where did their allegiances lie?

I ask the unthinkable.

"Was Ota a Nazi?"

"No, we weren't Nazis," she reassures me.

I release the breath I have been holding and let her continue.

"What did we have to do with Germany? We were here in Yugoslavia. Who was going to work and defend our farms if the men went off to fight?"

I push her again. I really do not want to go here.

"But there were some, weren't there?"

"There were some Nazi supporters in our town," she finally concedes. "That probably didn't help us. In the beginning, some men volunteered freely, but no men in our family enlisted. Toward the end when Germany was losing the war, they came and rounded up every last man that was still around—even the old and sick ones they could still find at home—and they took them with them on their last push."

"ICH ERKLAERE MICH FREIWILLIG"
(I DECLARE MYSELF FREEWILLING)

That's how the first recruitment acceptance form letters read. In the beginning years of the war, Germany's recruitment forces sought volunteers the world over. They especially played on the nationalistic pride in the minority Danube Swabians, whose ancestors had emigrated to eastern Europe from Germany 200 years before the war. In the rallies and town hall meetings, the Danube Swabian men heard words that lured some of them to battle. Like leaves on a blustery fall day, the Nazi propaganda flew about them.

In addition to the letters and visits from the recruiters and young soccer players, they were bombarded with Hitler's broadcasts on the radio. A prolific, charismatic speaker, he battered them nightly as they ate their evening bread. He fed them with siren songs of fear, racist superiority, intimidation, and brute force.

"Its (the state's) aim rests in the preservation and promotion of a community of physically and psychologically homogenous human beings."

"Whoever wants to live must therefore fight, and whoever does not wish to do battle, in this world of eternal struggle, does not deserve life."

"It is our wish and will that this Reich will last into the future for a thousand years."

"Long live national socialism. Long live Germany."

"Deutschland ueber Alles."

Over and over again. The dogs in the courtyard would join in the barking when they heard his voice on the wind.

Approximately 50 men from Kruschiwl—a town whose total population neared 950—enlisted freely in the German army. Most, like my mother's family, remained apolitical. They rejected the call to arms. For them, there was no imminent threat. Fighting had not reached their peaceful, pastoral fields. A harvest was upon them in the fall of 1944. And with the Reich government extending its long arm of control through the occupying Hungarian forces, they were lulled into a false sense of security. For a very short time, this simple minority could fly with the eagle.

You can see it in the photos. They learned how to mask. Like chameleons, they changed their skins. As many of their original family names were changed during the Hungarian Magyarization in 1865 to appeal to the then-controlling regime, they changed their faces in the late 1930's as well. Many men, including my grandfather and great uncle Jakob, began wearing that Hitler mustache. The sharp dark lines that extend down from the edge of the nostrils to rest heavily on the upper lip. A big black heavy rectangle, it looks like a voracious, decaying chipmunk tooth or a menacing black beak. No one looks friendly or handsome with that coal chip on his face. It doesn't flow with the curve of the lips the way a goatee can. Instead, it accentuates the hardness of the chin in a mean, unforgiving, uncompromising, razor-sharp, straight-to-hell kind of way.

Why, in heaven's name, did they choose to wear that?

"It was the style, then," my mother tells me.

Maybe so, but the pictures tell another side of the story. It bothers me to see these people I have loved emulating a man most of the world has villified as a monster. Although they won't admit it to me or anyone else, it horrifies me to think that they actually may have admired the man.

To wear a mustache to mask, to emulate, or to fit in is one thing. But to be pressured to fight in a war that one does not truly support is another. It was a difficult, complicated decision for most—and for many—one that was taken out of their hands.

After the First World War and the defeat of the Austria-Hungary empire, when Yugoslavia was newly created, the men of my grandfather's generation were first called to serve their military obligations. In 1927, my mother's uncle Jakob (*Jakobvetter*), served in the Yugoslavian army, and in 1929, my grandfather, Jacob, served his obligatory tour of duty. In 1941, when Germany took control of Belgrade, the Reich government awarded jurisdiction over Yugoslavia to its axis partner, Hungary. This area included Kruschiwl and all the towns and provinces extending north of Belgrade. Soon after this occurred, Hungary began drafting the young Swabian men into the Hungarian army. In 1942, after he was newly married, my mother's cousin, Adam, became one of the unlucky draftees.

EIN FREIWILLIGES MUSST (A FREEWILLING DUTY)

When 1944 arrived, and it was becoming apparent that Germany was losing the war, the call to fight took on a more strident, desperate tone. It was no longer a free-willing volunteerism; it became a free-willing must-do. A revised draft notice came in the mail, conscripting every last man—the sick or old notwithstand-ing—who was still left in the town. That is how my grandfather was called to report for duty.

But he never made it past the recruiting station beyond his introductory pro-cessing. Before the day came for him to leave, the partisans invaded and he was promptly deported to Russia as slave labor.

◆   ◆   ◆

He was drafted by the Hungarians. Deported by the Russians. Sacrificed by Yugoslavia in whose army he had served as a young man. And, never truly loved in the way a man dreams a woman will. What were my grandfather's allegiances? With his land gone and his family left to an uncertain fate, there were only two left and they could be found floating in a wine spritzer and a shot of schnapps.

I loved him for his weakness and his humanity. He gave me hope in the acceptance of imperfection. He taught me the art of compassion.

Eva Zettl, Katharina Zettl, Albert Zettl, and Jakob Zettl just before the
family was separated in Kruschiwl.

"Take this bread and eat of it. For this is my body,
which shall be given up for you and for all men,
so that sins may be forgiven."
(An excerpt from the Catholic Eucharistic Celebration)

July 9, 1997—A Visit to Jakobvetter

He is 82-1/2 years old with the face of a baby. Smooth, soft cheeks under round, smiling, boyish brown eyes. He is upbeat and personable despite the fact that just three months ago his dear wife and life partner of 63 years has left him on her transition to eternal life. I call him first to ask if he will speak to me about life in his hometown, before and after the war. These are both happy and sad memories, I have come to know. But this is a Danube Swabian, one of the most well-adjusted, strong, self-willed, loving people alive on this earth.

"Sure, Ingrid," he says, without skipping a beat.

The hardships have not changed this gracious man's sweet demeanor. Nothing, I'm convinced, will ever shake his calm and twinkling personality.

I arrive at his house at 2 p.m., our mutually agreed-upon time. After he gathers my hands in his and softly plants a kiss on my lips, as he has each and every time when greeting me over the years, I hand him a poppy seed strudel I have brought to sweeten any sadness that may bubble to the surface in our discussions. I bring him a peace offering—a taste of home he can savor with his memories. He places it in the kitchen for us to enjoy later, after we have spoken and I have taken a tour of his blooming vegetable garden and our appetites are sufficiently piqued for late afternoon *Kaffee und Kuchen*.

He returns to the living room and we settle in, I on a chair and he on the couch, his books and photo albums at easy arm's reach. He begins by telling me of life before the war, of his father's grandfather and the original settlers from Aleshausen, Germany who agreed to settle the land. These were the settlers that had come in the second wave of emigration that was promoted by Maria Theresia, after the Austria-Hungary empire defeated the Turks who then inhabited the area.

"I love reading about history," Jakobvetter confesses to me conspiratorially. "I'm, what do you say, a book worm."

He loses no time in describing the hearty ancestors who took up the royal offer to homestead what was once swampland in the Voyvodina and turn it into fertile waving fields of wheat and corn.

The ancestors came down the Danube River from Ulm, Germany in flat-bottomed boats they made from trees in the Black Forest. The boats were called *Ulmschachtel*, Ulm boxes. The journey was a one-way trip for them; once they arrived, they took the boats apart and used the wood to build their homes and heat their hearths. In the late 1700's, at about the same time America was being founded by the first English settlers, my ancestors came to Yugoslavia. Those who survived the attacks of Turks at the border and the malaria from the swamp mosquitoes that plagued them went on to transform the flat Pannonian Lowlands into a fertile breadbasket.

"My family had a 3,000 meter farm, which was all divided up equally between my brothers and sisters," he explained. "In March, we plowed. In April, we planted. From May through August, everything grew. In September, we harvested the corn. Afterwards, we planted the wheat. It lay dormant in winter and began growing in spring. We harvested wheat in June. To keep the soil healthy, we alternated planting the wheat and the corn between the two fields."

"We grew poppies at home, too," he tells me, nodding toward the kitchen where our poppy seed strudel sits on the counter.

They grew poppies and other things. Verdant fields of wheat and corn and barley and hemp and potatoes, tomatoes, peppers, and other kitchen vegetables. They had fruit trees for canning and grape vineyards that provided the family's own personal 100 liter wine allotment for the year.

"When I married, I was given my share of the land to farm. Kruschiwl was a small town, and when the time came, you usually knew who you would be matched up with. I was lucky. My wife, Eva, and I knew each other growing up and we always liked each other."

I wonder how much he must miss her now. There was always a compassion and kindness between them. He treated her with such deference and respect. I could tell he loved her by the way he held out his hands to her, palms always facing upward, open and trusting. He cooed about her; he loved the nest they made together. And, the passion—what a passion they had for each other. Their youngest child Eva was conceived in the labor camp they were deported to in Russia.

"When everything started unraveling," I asked, "why didn't you leave? I mean, you had radio and newspapers. You knew the Germans were losing the war and things might change."

"We didn't see any fighting in our town," he replies, "and we heard that people weren't doing too well in Germany and Austria."

Even though the war was all around them, they still felt safe in their little farming community. It hadn't touched them yet so they could still continue on with their lives—uninterrupted for now. So secure, and so adverse to change, they refused the German Army's offer to evacuate them on October 8, 1944.

In three, short weeks everything changed. The repercussions of the Yalta and Potsdam Conferences were becoming a reality; agreements made there by the Allies would doom them to be slave laborers for Russia and be expelled from their homelands. eastern Europe had had its fill of Germans and wanted them out. Like those of many townspeople, the lives of Jakob and his family would change forever. The next five years would bear witness to an entire family being torn apart, recreated, and reunited again.

"Do you remember the day when you saw Eva?" I ask, trying to imagine what it must have been like for Jakob, when he was finally released from Russia to join his wife in Dachau as a refugee. She had been released two years earlier, pregnant with Eva, his youngest child.

"Oh, ja," he tells me and smiles a smile from the inside, a memory for him alone. Later, his smile haunting me, I am left to imagine what his homecoming was like.

◆   ◆   ◆

On December 5, 1949, a young man of 31 named Jakob is released from a Russian labor camp and boards a train for Dachau, Germany. Once the site of a Nazi extermination camp, Dachau has now been converted into apartments to house the Danube Swabian refugees who have been released from labor and extermination camps in Russia and Yugoslavia. Dachau will be Jakob's new home. He is on a journey he has dreamed about and rehearsed in his mind night after night for almost two-years—to be reunited with his wife and the mother of his child he has never seen.

For almost three weeks, he gazes out at the changing landscape that moves slowly, much too slowly, past him. As the scenery rolls along before his eyes, his mind drifts back to that Christmastime of 1944 when his journey to Russia first began.

He is standing in the town square in his hometown of Kruschiwl with his wife Eva close by his side. They are surrounded by other similarly aged, able-bodied neighbors and friends whose faces are drawn and afraid on this cold and gray Christmas Day. All eyes are focused on the partisan soldier, with stars on the epaulets of his shoulders, a dark mustache that moves with the words on his lips.

As he listens, Jakob begins to realize that he and Eva and the others are human Christmas gifts. They are being given on this day not to their families and friends, but to these gruff soldiers who will take them to Russia to work in the coal mines and rock quarries. Strange—oh how strange it feels—to be standing here instead of in the warmth of his home, surrounded by his children, smelling the fresh goose that his wife would have been cooking when they got home from Christmas Mass. Instead, on this Holy Day, they are not in church, they are standing here in the cold, while partisan soldiers who have been gifted his home, are sitting at his table, eating fresh bread and warming their hands at his hearth. What gifts are these in store for Jakob and Eva?

It was only supposed to be for a few weeks. That's what they told them. A temporary work assignment to help the Russians get over the hump. Help them repair railroads, help them rebuild what the war had torn asunder. Just pack a few things, they said, you'll only be gone for a few weeks. And then you'll be home with your families.

But why do we have to leave now? What purpose does that serve? To tear us away from our loved ones during this special season? The children so look forward to Christmas, and now they will be left alone in the care of their grandparents. It is not right that we leave this day. But we have no choice. We are the vanquished, the victims, the stones in the path. And we are about to be kicked to the roadside by the black boots of revenge.

But what is that sound I hear now? The shuffling of our feet as we tread heavily, without hope, to catch our train to the unknown. The distant cries of the children are like birds on the wind, left alone in the nest, wondering when their parents will return with food in their beaks.

The people begin to move. One foot in front of the other. It is a sad, plodding rhythm, the sound feet make when they do not wish to leave. They begin the march away from all that is familiar and good to a lifetime of hard labor and uncertainty in a foreign land. When will he see his children again, he wonders, and he remembers crouching down in the doorway to hug them tightly. Before night falls, they walk the fifteen kilometers to the county seat in Sombor, where they are held in a large detention camp until the train arrives on January 13th to take them to Russia. They are herded again into cattle cars on a train not much different from the one he is on now.

Jakob looks down into his lap and stares at his hands. Hands that hold a lifetime of memories. Gnarled fingers, dry chapped skin and rough, sandpapery palms tell the tale of five long years of slave labor. He remembers the clanging jolting feel of the steel through his hands and arms as he chipped at the unforgiving stone in the rock quarries of Stalino.

How different the memory of the warmth and the damp softness of Eva's hand in his as they stood together on that first Christmas Day in Kruschiwl, when he put his arm around her and they began to walk away from the only life they had ever known. He remembers the feel of her hands wrapped around his neck at night when he sought her out and they comforted each other until dawn. His hands remember holding hers as she lay in the hospital bed in Russia after contracting typhus. The fleshy warmth transformed into thin, dry frail reeds in his hands.

He remembers the desperate fear that overtook him, trying to always hold on to her—her hands. Sometimes they are separated and the Russians use them as workers in other camps, but he pleads with the guards—pushes money into their hands—so that he and Eva can stay together. Sometimes he follows her. Sometimes she follows him. But it is always the same everywhere: the uncertainty of each day and whether or not it will be the last day that his fingers intertwine with hers.

He closes his eyes and feels her hands wrapped around his shoulders. The wetness of her tears on his cheek. The pulling away of the fingers over his palms as her train leaves to take her to the refugee camp in Dachau: a place of death where she will be able to recover from her illness and bring to term the new life that has dared to take shelter inside of her.

Jakob's hands have memories of being alone. For two more years they vibrate from chipping stone by day in the rock quarries. By night they are punctured with wooden slivers from building windows and doors for neighboring Russian families. His fingers know the grateful feeling of being able to fold over precious money earned by night, to hide it in the folds of undergarments, and to gladly hand it over to buy extra, lifesaving food.

On the train, Jakob's hands fidget with the threads of his clothing, flicking off idle specks and pulling at wayward threads. With these labored, loving, longing hands, he carefully smoothes down his shiny, black hair. He wants to be perfect when her eyes alight on him.

He watches the rugged coal mines of Russia flatten into the rich, rolling farmlands of Hungary and it reminds him longingly of his home. Even after all of this—the five years of captivity, the hunger, the separation, and the loneliness—he hates no one. Not the Serbs. Not the Russians. His only dislike is for the politics that drives people from their senses. He thanks God from the depths of his soul that he has kept his.

On Christmas Eve, almost exactly five years to the day Eva and he first departed for Russia, the train finally reaches Germany.

The train pulls into the station in Dachau and a young man's face is pressed against the windows, furtively looking out at visitors waiting to meet the passengers. His gaze flicks nervously from one face to the next. He eyes think they see familiar faces. Two women in beautiful coats huddle together, smiling and talking nervously. Could that be Eva and his sister, Helena? he wonders. It is cold and the warmth of his breath fogs up the window, and he finds himself in one moment alternately wiping away the fog with the sleeve of his jacket and fogging up the window with his eager face in the next. This goes on for several long, tortuous minutes. Finally the train's brakes squeal to a halt. His face feels a sudden cold rush of air, and his eyes can now see clearly for the first time.

A woman's high-pitched voice shouts out his name, and the sleeve of a beautiful coat raises in a wave. There are many Jakobs on this train, but he knows the call is meant for him and him alone. He looks up and sees Eva running to meet him. He moves quickly down the steps toward her. Eva's brown hair flies free from her kerchief, cheeks rosy from the cool brisk air. Suddenly, he feels his arms stretch out, a quick cold inward gasp of air enters his lungs and she is there in his arms—his hands on hers—and there is a power that envelopes them and holds them suspended in time and space. He kisses her and holds her tightly, presses her against his cheek, and his chest and his heart expands so they fill his throat with all the love he has held safely inside himself, and he feels her alive and full in his arms, and he is so happy that they are together again—alive and close and together again. It is—and remains—the happiest day of his life.

◆   ◆   ◆

When Jakob and Eva left Kruschiwl, they were forced to leave behind their two young children, Albert, age 5, and Kathe, age 2, in the care of Eva's mother. While Jakob and Eva toiled in the labor camp in Russia, the partisans took little Kathe and Albert away from their grandmother. According to communist plan, these 'orphans' were to be taken to state-run children's camps and orphanages, where they were to be raised as Serbian communists.

◆   ◆   ◆

"Don't take the children," my grandmother Helena implored her. "Go into the cornfields. Take them there and just wait a couple of hours and then come back to your house. It will be OK. Just don't take the children."

But the old woman had fear in her eyes. The kind of fear like window shades that pulls you down and covers up any sense of self determination or logic. The old woman had that distant, fixed look in her eyes, and in that moment Helena knew that she had lost her—had lost the children and would forever carry the guilt within her. But how could she calm the old woman's fear when she herself was fearful? What would happen to her brother's children now?

◆   ◆   ◆

Like cornstalks, they stood still in the town square holding their precious fruit in their arms. The old and fearful stand in the town square as the partisans have ordered.

"Bring us the children." *These orphans who are not yet orphans.* "Bring us the children."

She stands in the town square, holding the girl tightly to her breast to shield her from the cold. Little Kathe is bundled tightly in warm winter clothes. Silently she sleeps, innocent and unaware. In her right hand she holds the small hand of the boy, Albert. The wind blows the bangs of his white, blond hair, cut like a bowl around his face, framing round green eyes that look about at the other children, wide eyed and confused.

Why are we all here, he wonders. Why does grandmother hold my hand so tightly?

"You will give us the children," the partisan says. "You are not their parents, and you are too old to care for them properly. Their parents are now in Russia, and they may never return. We will take the children now and care for them. So it is ordered by Marshall Tito."

The old woman gasps and holds the children even tighter. She wants to turn and run to the corn fields now, but like the others, she is frozen in place. Frozen with fear. Cold despair fills her bones and Albert begins to whimper because her hand clutches his so hard it hurts.

Slowly, like the flapping sound of geese beginning their rise from a pond, a collective cacophony of cries begins to build and get stronger. The grandparents, distressed, begin their cries of lament, and the children, sensing the sudden danger, begin to cry. Albert stands close to her, wrapping his arms around her leg, hoping to hide behind her billowing, black skirt. She wraps her palm around his head, pressing his head harder against her thigh, and weeps.

They take the girl from her first. Easily, light as a feather, the precious bundle slips from her hands and is passed from one partisan hand to another. The partisankas are there to comfort the children and nestle them together in nearby wagons. It is harder to take the boy. He struggles and strives to hide, and she is helpless, reluctant to release him. He clutches her harder, pushing himself into her leg, hoping to disappear. But the partisan is stronger and more insistent. Soon the little boy's hand is in his, and he speaks softly to him as he moves him along and away to the wagon filling with boys.

"Come along, little one," he says. "Come and take a ride with your other friends here."

Albert walks away from her obediently but looks over his shoulder to see his grandmother one last time. Round, green, hollow eyes stare forlornly to see her openmouthed, tear-streaked face in shock. Suddenly her load is lighter, her arms are empty, and her hands are clutched tightly at her sides as if still holding the boy. The heaviness of the sudden void presses upon her heart, and she stands motionless until she is told to go.

A partisan soldier touches her arm and rouses her from her trance.

"Go home, now," he urges. "Go home, now, Swabian."

She begins to totter and sway and stumble along, still feeling the warmth of the boy pressed against her thigh. *What will happen to them now? Will I ever see them again?* Thoughts of despair cloud her vision as she plods along. With empty hands and an empty heart, she begins her walk away from life, away from the children and all that is good and light and hopeful. The darkness of the day falls upon her, and on that day she begins to die.

◆   ◆   ◆

Kathe

The children are separated and placed in communist children's orphanages—Kathe in a girl's facility and Albert with other boys—where they are schooled in Serbian and indoctrinated to become good janissaries for Tito. Kathe remembers being in two state-run orphanages. The first one was in Starchivo where she spent two years studying with the kindergartners. Then she was transferred to Ulmja where she spent another two years.

The teachers in the state-run schools encourage the students to study well. All school work is to be done in honor of Tito. Kathe remembers hearing the teachers give motivational speeches to encourage socialism. There is never any religious study taught there.

She is treated well by the older Serbian girls who take care of her and the other children. Clothed and fed well, she grows to love her caretakers, Katiza and Veritza Mladewovitz.

"They were family to me," Kathe tells me. "They loved and took care of me, and I loved them. I didn't even know my parents anymore. I was so young when I was taken."

"Did you ever have visitors?" I ask.

"I remember once this man—he wasn't my father—throwing me up in the air and laughing. I laughed with him. He was a nice man, but he wasn't my father. This Serbian couple wanted to adopt me. But, then, that's what they did to us—they adopted us out to childless couples. The adoption was stopped, though, because my grandmother, who had learned of my whereabouts, came to visit me. She informed the authorities that she had been in contact with my parents in Russia by letter, and that they were still alive and would likely return."

"What do you think your life would have been like had you been adopted?"

"I have no idea. Totally different, I'm sure. And I probably wouldn't have emigrated to the United States. But, then again, knowing what has taken place in Yugoslavia over the last 50 years, you just never know."

"How long were you in Ulmja?"

"I didn't leave Ulmja until 1951 when I was nine years old. I didn't know my brother, Albert, either, because we had been separated all that time. Even though we were placed on the same train when they released us, they put us in separate sections. He was with the boys in one car, and I was with the girls in another. I didn't see him until we arrived in Austria."

"Tell me about the time you saw my mother at the train station."

"The train stopped in Salzburg on its way to Germany, and my Aunt Helena and Cousin Mary were there to greet me. They picked me right out of the crowd, and they knew Albert, too. Even though we had been in Yugoslavia for almost seven years, they still knew us. We hadn't changed that much. It probably helped because we had a family portrait taken before my parents were deported to Russia. My father, mother, Albert, and I. Aunt Helena probably had a copy."

"Your mother was nice to me. She spoke to me in Serbian at the train station. I didn't know a word of German anymore. I wanted to stay with her and Aunt Helena that day, but I had to get back on the train and go to Germany where my parents were waiting."

"What do you remember about your brother, Albert?"

"I saw him for the first time during our stopover in Salzburg. He was 12 years old then and so very blond. I am just the opposite. My hair is dark and my eyes are brown. I'll never forget the first words he spoke to me when he saw me. He called me *Ziganka*. It means gypsy. And I took one look at his white, blond head, and I called him *Kosa,* which means goat. So that's how our relationship as brother and sister began. Calling each other nicknames I still remember to this day."

"Tell me about your arrival in Dachau."

"The train finally arrived in Dachau where my parents lived in the refugee camp. When my parents saw Albert and me, they were overcome with emotion. They hugged us tightly, but I felt strange and distant from them. I didn't even know them anymore. All I knew was that I had been taken away from my Serbian family at the orphanage, and I was very sad and confused."

"What was it like living in Dachau?"

"My parents didn't keep me at home for very long before they sent Albert and me to the *Umschullung*. The Umschullung was a school that they sent all of the children to who had been schooled in Serbian orphanages. At the Umschullung, we were taught to be Germans again. It was a sort of immersion school. We couldn't speak anything but German there."

"The Umschullung was in a place called Bernried. Bernried is near the Stanberger See, about 20 miles south of Munich. It was a beautiful place, and the school itself had once been a medieval castle. At Bernried, I received religious instruction for the very first time, which I really enjoyed. It is there that I experienced my First Holy Communion."

"After spending a year at Bernried, I was finally able to go home to get to know my parents. At the time, people who had had children in Serbian orphanages were sending them to another place after the Umschullung. This place was sort of a spa. It was supposed to help us more. But I didn't want to go, even though my parents were considering it. I just wanted to stay put for awhile and get to know them. They must have agreed because I never went there to recuperate. I spent the next six years in Germany going to school and becoming a teenager. In December of 1958, when I was 16-1/2 years old, my family emigrated to the United States."

Albert

Kathe's brother, Albert, is a toe-head. Hair so white it glistens like fine new straw in the startling sunlight. That must be where my brother's children get their bright blond hair from. Albert moves freely under the glow of his natural spotlight; see how he laughs and runs and kicks his soccer ball, sending out sparklers from his head like a brilliant birthday cake ablaze.

Sometimes he suffers under the glare of his white-capped, Aryan beauty. Wide, full-fleshed cheeks around deep-set green eyes, eyes with the long, luxuriously sweeping lashes that boy children are often blessed with. Even at six years of age, his suspect beauty is enough to unleash the dogmatic bigotry of the teachers in this state-run, Serbian orphanage for boys—this school where the sons of the deported Danube Swabian slave laborers are placed alongside those of their fallen partisan brethren.

Unlike his sister, Kathe, with her dark, gypsy-like looks, Albert—the little, snow-white-haired goat—suffers unfairly in the boy's orphanage. He tries not to remember—tries harder not to speak of it—but with constant nudging he sheds a little light into the dark corner of his childhood pain.

What did they do him there?

They singled him out unfairly and took opportunities to do so when he was acting out and misbehaving. They shoved him out of the game, out of the line. Made him stand alone. Humiliated him and alienated him in front of the other children. This evil little German boy. They made him an example for the others. Made him stand alone and suffer under the glare of his own bright headlight.

The boy's orphanages were miserable places, Albert tells me. It was like being in the Army: very regimented, orderly, and strict—the very antithesis of a little boy's life. Up early every morning to line up in formation. Exercise. Eat. Go to classes. Study. And play soccer. Ah, soccer.

He loved to run and play soccer. Suntanned, strong brown legs pumping under him, pivoting with ease over a soccer ball. His left foot sets the ball before him; his right leg kicks it out far and away. Goal.

What was the goal of this little lost, not-yet orphan boy? What was his dream, his overriding wish? To run. To make his great escape away from the orphanage and away from the pain. To follow his soccer ball and run far, far away.

His bright, white, little-boy light is moved to three different schools and one sanitarium in several different towns from the time he is six to 12 years old. It begins in Kanjisa, a town closest to where he lived as a boy. Between the ages of six to nine, he contracts tuberculosis and is placed temporarily in a sanitarium located somewhere on the Theiss River until he recovers. Later on he is moved farther away to the middle of the Batschka to a town called Srbobran. Finally, he ends up in a school in Novisad, the biggest town of the three.

He was just a little boy. A blond, unkempt, little boy who was picked on by the bigger boys and needled into many fist fights. He was just a little boy who squirmed in family portraits and frustrated the best of photographers. He was just a little boy who liked to climb up on the front door of the house until his grandparents would yell for him to get down. He was just a little boy who teased goats and was knocked down by an old ram who butted him over and over again. He was just a little boy—the apple of his mother's eyes—whose eyes he could no longer remember smiling at him with love. He was the only living son of parents who now struggled to stay alive in Russia, even though they were already dead to him in memory.

Every so often he gets visitors. His grandmother and grandfather set out one day in search of the lost children. They walk from town to town making inquiries.

"Look here," she points with gnarled fingers to a creased family photo that he pulls out from inside his coat pocket. "Look here. Have you seen this little, blond-haired boy and his dark-haired sister?"

The picture is pulled out many times and shown to many school officials in the towns known to have children's schools. The picture is the family portrait that was taken shortly before their own child—the children's mother—was deported to Russia. This is the picture that was so hard for the photographer to take because the little boy would not sit still.

"Are the children here?" Albert's grandparents ask hopefully of each orphanage's authorities.

And they point to the picture with hope in their hearts until one day they are told *yes,* and the little boy is allowed to get visitors—familiar faces from home—a lost place of safety and love—far, far away. His grandmother, vindicated again, finds her lost prize, and with a sigh of relief, takes a living breath again.

◆   ◆   ◆

From Germany, Jakob and Eva began the work of reuniting their family again. They enlisted the assistance of Archbishop Rohracher, the archbishop of Salzburg, who worked with the German Red Cross to reunite the families of refugees. Through the archbishop's help, Jakob, Eva, and my grandmother, who still suffered from the guilt of not being able to convince Eva's mother to hide the children in the cornfields, worked tirelessly to locate and extradite the children from their respective orphanages.

Of the 40,000 children who were taken from the Danube Swabians when they were deported to Russia, 35,000 were placed into communist children's orphanages. It was assumed that 5,000 of the older children, aged 8-12 years old, were too old to be raised as Serbians and were, therefore, killed in deportation centers, such as Derventa Doboj-Usora, in the local sugar refinery.

Finally, in 1951, Kathe and Albert joined the ranks of the 5,000 children who were located and reunited with their families in Germany and Austria. It is assumed that the remaining 30,000 children, who were unaccounted for, were adopted and raised by Serbians.

Rosalia and Adam Szettele on their wedding day in Kruschiwl.

*"We didn't get very much food to eat in the camp.
We got two pieces of bread to eat. One in the morning and one at night."*

Adam Szettele

September, 1997

Adam, Sali, and I meet one late morning in early fall. This is a tenuous meeting, and an opportune one for me, and I am well aware that it may have never occurred save the luck fate had dealt me.

Weeks earlier, when it was still summer, I had been at Jakobvetter's, and we had just finished our *Kaffee* and *Kuchen* and were sitting in the living room looking through some old family photo albums. We were going through Tante Eva's *Totesbuch,* a photo album filled with the photos of deceased relatives. Strange pictures, these, some showing the long faces of loved ones, gazing down sad-eyed into corpse-filled caskets, and others depicting only black and white close-ups of the dead. Strange pictures, these European artifacts, that prove beyond a shadow of a doubt that the face of death should remain foreign and not pretty to behold.

I had just been informed that Jakob and Eva had two other children that never lived. One died at birth and the other, whose face looks out at me from a casket instead of a crib, was only one-and-a-half when he died. The baby, who looks asleep, is surrounded by a much younger, mustachioed Jakob and the sorrow-filled face of a younger, plumper Eva.

"This baby was such a good, happy baby," says Jakob, "always laughing and smiling."

Like many infants in Kruschiwl in the 20's who did not live to their toddler years, the baby took ill with pneumonia, then a fatal, untreatable disease. The realization that Jakob and Eva actually had five children, instead of the three that I know, is dawning on me when suddenly the sound of the back door opening rouses us from our somber moods. A bass-voiced *halloo* accompanies it, and in the next moment my Uncle Adam appears.

He has just stopped in to see Jakob and is surprised to see me there. Jakob explains that we are talking about the history of the Danube Swabian emigration to Yugoslavia and the years he spent in Russia and suddenly, from some magical and far away place, Adam's voice begins to run like a babbling brook. Words come spilling out about how he was released from the Russian prison camp, and an incredible saga of a dangerous border crossing spills forth.

His words tumble out—people, places, horses, gunshots—an emotional tale with memory skipping over the details of a near-death experience like water over the boulders in a kayak run. I am amazed by what I am hearing, and I thank my lucky stars. Jakob, ever the gracious host, turns the conversation over to Adam and lets him release this torrential outpouring of his life.

I question Adam about his experience, and he gifts me with yet another wonderful surprise.

"Come over and see me," he says. "We'll talk some more. I'll tell you all about Russia and what happened there."

I can't believe my good fortune. I thought I was destined to never hear his tale. When I first called to meet with Adam—it was weeks before my meeting with Jakobvetter—Adam's wife Sali answered the phone.

"I've decided to write about what happened in Kruschiwl and Russia, and I was hoping to talk with you and Adam to get more information."

She wasn't up for it, though. She wanted no part of it.

"It is better to leave the past where it is," she somberly stated.

I tried again.

"Well, what if we just talked about the town and what is was like growing up there. The lifestyle. The way the farms were laid out."

This city girl from Chicago has no clue about farming.

"No, Ingrid. *No,*" she replied with that characteristic, choppy nervous laugh of hers. For some, I would come to learn, there are no safe topics where Kruschiwl is concerned.

So, here I am, finally surprised and delighted to find myself at the table, this place I was always meant to be. I turn on the cassette recorder I have brought with me, and Adam begins his transformation back in time.

I learn how a man grows up in a small town. He builds a wooden sawhorse and rides it in the barn when he is a boy. He works in the fields with his father when he is older. And, whenever he walks past his childhood sweetheart's house, just two doors away, he notices how pretty she is whenever he catches her eye.

Sali laughs nervously and gets up to serve coffee but lets Adam continue telling his tale. The hours slip by, and with the appearance of a table setting before us, I can tell that Adam and I have talked our way to the lunch hour.

At the kitchen counter, Sali slices a loaf of French bread and places it on a plate nearby. A lid is removed from a pot on the stove and the familiar aroma of beef goulash greets me. I get up to peek inside. Stewed beef, *Spaetzle* noodles, and potatoes in a tasty paprika-spiced sauce. Sali shoos me back to the table, and she places the bread, a bowl of goulash, and a sour-cream and cucumber salad before me. *Mmmmm.* This lunch is a throwback to Danube Swabian farming days that begin at five o'clock in the morning and go on until dusk. Adam and I look at each other and I click off the microcassette, gazing at the goulash expectantly.

"Go on, Ingrid. Eat." Sali encourages me with a smile.

Afterwards, our stomachs full and our spirits fortified, Adam tells me his tale of survival and a border crossing nearly missed.

◆   ◆   ◆

In April of 1941 when Hitler bombed Belgrade, World War II reached Yugoslavia and Kruschiwl fell under the domain of Hungary. In October of 1942, after Adam and Sali were newly married, he was drafted into the artillery unit of the Hungarian army in the city of Sombor. In August of 1944, he was assigned to fight on the east front near Czechoslovakia. On April 20, 1945, his unit surrendered, and he became a Russian prisoner of war. He was incarcerated in a concentration camp in Siberia and was put to forced labor in coal mines and rock quarries. After two hard years in the camps, on July 7, 1947, he was released.

The guards asked him where he wanted to be transported.

"Yugoslavia," he stammered. "I am Yugoslavian."

He was afraid to say he was German, and he wanted to go back to the land of his birth. At the time, he had no idea what kind of transformation had taken place in the towns of the Batschka. He just wanted to go home. The guards put him on a transport that took him to a huge camp in Subotica that was filled with Germans. There he learned that his beloved Kruschiwl had been turned into a concentration camp. It was then he realized what a mistake he had made by not requesting a transport to Germany.

"Oh, no, what did I do now? What was I thinking when I told the Russians that I was Yugoslavian?"

Adam soon discovered that his homecoming would be spent alone. While he was a prisoner of war in Russia, his parents had left Kruschiwl for Germany, and his wife had been deported to Russia and was working in Stalino, thousands of miles away.

After three days in the camp at Subotica, wondering what he could do or where he could go, soldiers appeared and asked for three men to volunteer to ride horses to Gakowa.

"They needed men who knew how to ride horses, and I grew up riding horses as a child, so I volunteered. Also, I knew that Gakowa was only three miles away from Kruschiwl, and I wanted to go to see if I could see anyone I knew from my town. Each man was to ride one horse and pull along two others."

"Sure enough, we passed Kruschiwl and there I saw Rosi's (Sali's) parents and her brother and the old folks. When they saw me, they were screaming and crying. The guards only gave me two minutes to hug and kiss them before I had to get back on the horse and keep going. Somehow, through the barbed-wire fence, my mother-in-law managed to slip me 200 dinars."

"In Gakowa, the guards let us free in the camp there for the night and told us that we had to meet at a certain corner in the morning, and then we would take the train back to Subotica. In the morning, I didn't go back, but I was very worried because I wasn't registered there to receive food rations."

"Later that night in the camp in Gakowa, I talked to a woman who told me about a guide who just that night was organizing an escape for a group of about 100 prisoners. This guide would arrange everything and bribe the guards so we could get out of the camp. There was only one problem. He wanted 800 dinars a person and I only had the 200 my mother-in-law gave me the day before in Kruschiwl."

"Then this woman came up with another idea. There was an old man in the camp with one foot, she said, who needed help. He needed someone to carry his backpack on our escape. I was able-bodied, so I figured I could do that. In return for my help, he would pay the guide the 800 dinars for me to get out."

"Around eight or nine o'clock that night when it turned dark, we began to follow our guide out of the camp. I had the heavy backpack on, and our group started to walk. We looked like a long row of goslings, following our mother goose. Some of us were already out of the camp near the corn fields; others were just getting out of the camp; and more, still, were just starting out when an alarm sounded. The guards started shooting, running about and shouting for us to stop."

"I was in a dried-up drainage ditch on the outskirts of camp when all the commotion started. Two corn fields bordered the ditch, one ahead of me on a steeper incline and one behind me and off to the left, closer to the camp. I tried to move ahead to climb out of the drainage ditch, but the weight of the backpack kept holding me back. I stumbled and fell several times. Finally, I took the backpack off to try again, but by then it was too late."

"The guards were close by now and I had to crawl back and into the corn fields to my left. I sat there scared and didn't move for hours, so the corn wouldn't rustle. When the patrolling soldiers finally left, I made my way carefully back to camp. That's when I learned we had been cheated. Our guide never paid the guards to arrange our smooth escape. Instead, he kept the money and got away himself."

Back at the camp in Gakowa, Adam sought the help of the woman again. She had yet another idea.

"On the next morning, I was to ride with a man to a farm just outside of camp and help him load straw on his wagon. I climbed on, and we went our way. At the farm, I loaded the straw and then we waited for my *doppelgaenger* to arrive. My double had been begging in another town, and when he finally arrived, he jumped on the wagon in my place and those two went back to camp, leaving me alone by some corn fields."

"Two men left the camp and another two came back in. That's all the guards knew to check identity. Two out, two in. I was now free of the camp in Gakowa, standing alone on the outside in broad daylight. I knew I couldn't do much until nightfall except get out of sight."

"It was August then, and the corn was already high, so I slipped into the corn fields and lay down for a nap. I was tired, and I slept a long time. When I awoke, I didn't know where I was at first. I could see that it was dark, but not too dark. I roused myself and started to move. I decided to go back first to Kruschiwl to pick up Rosi's mother, brother, and the grandparents, but when I got there the police dogs started barking, and the guards began shooting. It was too dangerous to do anything. I couldn't rescue them. So, there I was, scared and alone in a corn field outside of the Kruschiwl camp. I made up my mind to go to Hungary by myself. Hungary was only four kilometers away."

"I made my way through border farms and navigated by counting corn fields. I knew there were about four or five fields I had to go through before I reached the border. I walked alongside the corn counting so I could keep the rustling noise to a minimum, but yet I was close enough to jump back in if I needed to get under cover quickly. The moon was shining full and I was careful to walk outside of the light."

"Soon I reached the border and saw two guards waiting for me. I took cover in the corn and peered out every so often to see what was going on. Somehow the guards must have seen me or heard me. I was so close, I thought I could just take a step over the border, somehow through the corn. But it was no use. They were waiting for me to come out, which I eventually did. I was thinking, should I go forward or back, I'll probably be killed anyway. I finally decided to surrender. Hands up in the air, I came out of the corn and started walking towards them."

"One guard frisked me, and the other shouted for me not to move. In Serbian he said, 'Don't move. Otherwise I won't shoot you right, and you'll just suffer needlessly.' When they asked me where I was going, I made up a story and said that I was trying to get home. I told them that my wife was Hungarian and I made a mistake by coming to Yugoslavia. I don't know if they believed me or not, but they made me walk a gauntlet to the guard station at the border. The guard station was about three kilometers away, and at every 100 meter interval where a guard was stationed, I got a painful rifle butt in the back. They kept hitting me until I could barely walk anymore. Just kill me now and be done with it, I'm thinking. Once I reached the border station, I joined a large group of other people, like me, who had also escaped the camps, only to be captured again at the border. I talked to a guard, who seemed like a nice fellow, and I asked him what I could do. I offered him the 200 dinars that my mother had given me in exchange for my freedom."

"You don't have to do anything," he replied. "At 12 o'clock midnight, the lieutenant will come and release you."

"That's bullshit, I'm thinking, but sure enough at midnight this officer comes and checks us all out. He gathers the group of us together and intimidates everyone into giving up any valuables they may still have on them. At first, he didn't get very much. But then they found a watch that one man was hiding, and they beat him up pretty bad for not giving it up. You should have seen all the watches and money, too, that started flying out after that. That's where I lost the 200 dinars my mother-in-law gave me. I gave up the money, but I kept my wedding ring. I don't remember where I put it, probably in my mouth or somewhere else. You wouldn't believe where we put things."

"Afterwards, the high ranking officer took us to a forest and told us to walk 100 meters ahead. To the very end I thought we were just going to be shot there. But we were just told to walk the short distance through the woods and soon enough we crossed the border and we were in Hungary."

"What was happening in Hungary?" I ask.

"Everything was OK there. You had to know someone to find work somewhere. My dad's father was already there. And my mother was there, too. She left Kruschiwl about a year before, but her folks stayed behind. People were afraid to go. You never knew if it was better to stay or to leave. I always say that whoever stayed alive did the right thing in the end."

I take a deep breath.

"How did you keep your wedding ring?" I finally ask.

"In the Russian labor camp, where I was prisoner of war, I had to work in coal mines and rock quarries, chipping rocks in the bitter cold Siberian winter. It was very hard work, and we got very little to eat. When we came in from the cold, no one would get undressed. We just opened our coats and shook the lice out and buttoned up again. Occasionally, we had to strip naked and go into a bath to be deloused. The guards would take our clothes, and we would sit on the ground and I would dig a whole and put my ring inside. It was a tricky thing. You had to remember the exact position where you buried it. While we were being deloused, a guard would come into our quarters with a metal rod and prod the earth until he heard a clink of metal. It was easier to find watches—they were bigger, easier to locate—but a ring was harder. Even if your stick went through the ring, you would miss it. It was very difficult to just hit upon the edge of a thin ring band."

"I was lucky in a way. I always kept my ring. And I could have exchanged it for a lot of bread. But I hung on to it. I always thought, things could get worse. I had a lot of self-control. I'm not saying that's the right thing to do. It's just something I did. I held on to my ring all those five, long years. And I still wear it today."

◆   ◆   ◆

Within months of his arrival in Hungary, Adam left to reunite with Sali in Graz, Austria. They went about the business of rebuilding their lives together after having been separated for the better part of the first five years of their marriage. In 1949, their daughter Katharina (Kathi) was born. As a family, they emigrated to the United States in 1957.

PART III
From Refugees to Immigrants ~ The Journey to America

Due to the lack of work in postwar Germany and Austria, and the large numbers of refugees there, American and French politicians recommended liberal emigration to other countries. Private humanitarian organizations also helped by waging campaigns to raise sympathy for those fleeing from communism. Thanks to their collective efforts, Congress passed the Displaced Persons Act of 1948, which allowed 400,000 dislocated refugees to emigrate to the United States. In 1950, an American congressional committee recommended that one million German expellees should emigrate.

In Salzburg, Austria, my mother and her family were encouraged to apply to this immigration program and were accepted. In 1951, they saw the Statue of Liberty for the first time, and in 1957, they became citizens of the United States.

Mathias Thoebert, Helena Thoebert, Katharina Burlem, Jacob Thoebert, and Maria Andor with baby daughter, Ingrid.

"I was raised to get by on a very little. One change of clothing was sufficient. You washed it out and you wore it. The partisans used to say, 'We take everything away from them and they still look clean and presentable.' We were raised that way. We didn't need much to get by. We kept ourselves in order."

Maria Andor

Citizenship Day—July 16, 1957

In the picture that I have, they all look happy. Every single one of them—*Four Generations Represented,* blares the headline—has a big smile on their face. My Aunt Kathy looks absolutely ecstatic; her eyes still sparkle in the yellowing and dog-eared newsprint, and her mouth is wide open. Her lips, which moments earlier had just spoken the Oath of Allegiance, are now spread in a show-all-teeth grin that says, *Hey. Look at that. We did it!* My Grandfather, Jacob, looks relieved and grateful to be getting another round at US citizenship; he has the flush of newborn patriotism on his face. My Great Grandfather Mathias' smile is wide and loose and casually relaxed. He doesn't look at all perturbed by the thought that had he not taken his family back to Yugoslavia in 1921, maybe all the suffering they would have had to endure was the Depression. My Grandmother Helena's smile is polite, with an underlying note of 'glad that it's finally over,' and my mother's smile is a little unsure about what comes next; she looks bemused—or embarrassed perhaps—at the reporter's sudden interest. Aside from my mother, who is holding me in her arms, everyone is holding up the precious Certificate of Citizenship high overhead in their right hands: the folder that has the big block two-dimensional letters USA on the front.

The article below the pictures reports that three generations of my family had spent four years as prisoners of the *Russians.* It also mentions that my Great Grandfather Mathias first came to the US in 1907 but returned to *Austria* in 1921, when my Grandfather Jacob was 15, to *save the family farm.* Some of these details are slightly askew.

My mother, grandmother, aunt and great grandparents were actually prisoners of the communist partisans in Yugoslavia, while my Grandfather Jacob and my Father Henry—who is not present in the photo but already a citizen—were interned in Russian forced labor camps. Great Grandfather Mathias returned to *Yugoslavia* in 1921, since the country had already been parceled away from the Austria-Hungary Empire and recreated as Yugoslavia in 1918 after the First World War. As far as *saving the family farm* after 14 years is concerned, I rather believe it is more correct to assume that his motives were to save himself and get out of the city and back to his homeland and his true love of farming. There are only so many tomato plants you can cultivate on a 9'x 3' strip of dirt along a fence that borders a city alley in Chicago. And, while he was at it, he might as well take his teenage son back home and have him hitched to a nice Danube Swabian girl. To me, the article is more fascinating for what it does not say—the dramas of life that it evokes beyond the hidden curtain of the written page, which reveals nothing but the basic *facts*.

On July 16, 1957, my great grandfather, my grandfather, my grandmother, my aunt, and my mother all earned what had been automatically bestowed on me 18 months earlier at birth: their US citizenship. It took me 40 years to discover that July 16, 1957 was the single most important day of my life.

It meant that I would grow up to be an American—to live in a country where I could choose a creative way of life. I would not be marked by the farm like my forebears had been. I would not be raised to be a farmer's wife or learn how to strangle a chicken's neck for the evening meal like my grandmother had done. I could wear Capri pants and roller blade instead of donning a big black hoop skirt and a heavy black babushka to fry duck's blood. I could stay single and childless and smoke if I felt like it. I could sit at my kitchen table and watch the rain through the Pella sliding glass door blur the boughs on the old blue Spruce and not worry about putting dinner on the table at all. I could change my life at 40, start doing yoga, give myself biceps for Christmas at a health club, instead of at a threshing machine, and wear extended contact lenses to my heart's content. I could grow up in a big city and expand my thoughts and options to include writing about the woman who held me in her arms that day while I squinted out into the midday July sun.

Unlike that woman I would learn to call Mother, I could grow up feeling relatively sure that I could not be spending my teenage years as a prisoner of communist partisans. I could feel relatively safe knowing that—barring my refusal to pay my mortgage, my taxes, or having my house situated on the fast lane of a future expressway—no rising star of a dictator would evict me from my home and dispossess me of my assets, my identity, and my citizenship. I would remain who I was, or who I chose to create myself to be, at will. The decision would not be thrust upon me; I would hold the key to my own makeover.

One year ago, I took the key into hand, and the little girl turned from the camera to face her mother and squint into her face for the very first time.

◆   ◆   ◆

One day after their naturalization (*Interesting word, don't you think? Were they unnatural before being sworn in?*), three Chicago daily newspapers all carried their citizenship day story, and two of them printed photographs. Was it because in 1957, America still had a fascination with and acceptance of immigrants, especially refugees that had been interned in concentration camps and forced to endure the hardships of slave labor at the hands of the communists? Was it a color-me-red, oh horrors, land-of-the-free, aren't-we-cool thing? Or was it because America—like it usually does—was still basking in the savior-of-the-world syndrome. The, oh, what the heck, let's just open our doors wide and relax those immigration policies of post World War II?

Or, maybe America felt a measure of responsibility in having played a part in the need to loosen them in the first place. Perhaps America was admitting its complicity at the Yalta and Potsdam conferences, which condoned the mass expulsions, slave labor as *war reparations,* and the refugee trek of millions of displaced ethnic Germans into depressed areas of Europe.

The world was fearful, that with the lack of work and the sudden overcrowding, the depressed conditions in the war-torn countries of Germany and Austria could and would prove to make a powerful breeding ground for communism. Golly gee, didn't America have a part in creating the Cold War, and weren't we trying to help ease this new problem with the same fear we used in battling the old one? We got those damn Germans out of eastern Europe, now we'd better get them the hell out of Germany. You know, that kind of thing.

Whatever—they let them in. They let them out of those refugee camps in Germany and Austria, which were nothing but old Nazi horse barns and remodeled holocaust ovens, and they finally let them in and gave them a chance. They gave me a chance, too. Do they ever realize how many generations—how many individual souls—they benefit? If they did, they'd probably put aside their fears and tear that steel wall down in Texas as fast as they could mobilize the National Guard.

◆   ◆   ◆

Maybe I should be thankful that guilt played a part in easing the post World War II immigration policies. Collective guilt is a powerful thing. It played a part in putting my family in their mess in the first place, and by the same token, it helped to take them out. The world was reeling from the horrors of the Holocaust, and like a wounded child, it needed to lash out with revenge and retribution. So, when the German Reich was invaded at the very farthest reaches, in the most vulnerable areas of East Prussia, in the Sudetenland of Czechoslovakia, and in the small farming communities of Yugoslavia and Romania, the backlash dramatically altered the lives of ethnic German minorities, like my mother's and her family's.

Largely apolitical farmers, their lives were overtaken. They were imprisoned in concentration camps and forced to endure slave labor prior to being expelled. *Why?* When you strip away all of the historical and political mambo, it comes down to this: they were ethnic Germans, they were hated; they were minorities, they were vulnerable; and they would be the first to suffer German collective guilt over the Holocaust. Not even Hitler's folly could escape the Law of Cause and Effect.

In the years immediately preceding and following the war's end, 14 to 15 million ethnic Germans were expelled from their central and eastern European homelands. The vast majority of refugees streamed into Germany and Austria. Many of them stayed there in the refugee camps for a few years to get back on their feet. They worked on farms, in factories, and like my Uncle Jakob, they employed their construction skills to help with the rebuilding of Germany—a feat that was accomplished in three, short years. But jobs, food, and housing were scarce, and they were not welcomed in what was once falsely proclaimed to be their Fatherland.

During the tumultuous decade after World War II, it appeared as if all of Europe were in transit. The ethnic Germans, who began the exodus, made up 1/3 of the 45 million people who were displaced under duress after 1945. Clearly, something had to be done.

Thanks to the efforts of private humanitarian organizations, like the National Catholic World Conference (NCWC), which waged campaigns to raise sympathy for those managing to flee from communism, Congress passed the Displaced Persons Act of 1948. The Act allowed 400,000 refugees who had been dislocated to emigrate to the U.S. It made it possible for my father to get off a plane at

O'Hare airport in his cousin's hand-me-down coat in 1949. Then, in 1951, one year after an American congressional committee recommended the immigration of one million German expellees, my mother was allowed to take a choppy cruise on the General Taylor, come face to face with the State of Liberty, and eventually smile at a reporter on the steps of the Federal Building on a warm day in Chicago in July of 1957.

◆   ◆   ◆

Why are immigration policies so restrictive anyway? Could it be that they are built on fear by fiercely nationalistic societies that hold homogeneity of the population and their economic protection in high regard?

Some of the more common arguments against U.S. immigration include:

"Foreigners will ruin our economy by working for such low pay that they will hold down wages for working people overall." Even worse, there is this one: "They take all of the jobs away from Americans, especially minorities." And then, there's this one: "Immigrants are overly dependent on U.S. welfare programs and are raising their children and receiving medical care on the public dole."

What I have observed as the child of immigrants goes like this: when you don't have anything and you're starting from scratch, you work for what you can get. It's an issue of relativity; something is better than nothing. Because many immigrants have language and educational deficiencies, they usually get the low-paying, menial jobs: assembling parts in factories, cleaning houses and businesses, and being nannies for wealthy physicians and businessmen and their families. These are not exactly the jobs every American dreams of when asked what they want to be when they grow up. My mother did them all. She worked in factories and she cleaned houses and she was grateful to get the work.

As far as living on the public dole is concerned, my parents never collected a dime of welfare, and they were proud of that fact. In 1951, immigrants were expected to be assisted by their sponsors and their own resourcefulness borne out of necessity. They came to Chicago because jobs were plentiful then. Anyone with a will to work could find a job, English speaking or not, college educated or not, white collar or not.

Opponents of immigration argue that immigrants today, who are largely from Asia and Latin America, are different from those Europeans, like my parents, who immigrated in the 1950's. I don't know about that; deep down, hungry, tired, poor, desperate, how different are people, really? But, as in every strata of society, there appears to be a pecking order among immigrants, too. Who's more white?

Who's more educated? Who will assimilate better? That's another issue, and it's someone else's story to tell. All I can say is, I'm glad for my sake as well as theirs, that the door was opened for my family.

It's one thing to speak in generalities and present arguments and statistics, and it's another to look into the faces of people who have been displaced under duress. So, let's get back to the picture where they look so happy to be given this opportunity to be Americans. They are real people—*natural* people—after all, even if they spell funny and speak an accented English. Let the woman that holds me in her arms tell you how she became a refugee and an immigrant in the first place.

◆   ◆   ◆

How We Got Out of Kruschiwl

"After a couple of years, even the partisans grew tired of the camps. They began to turn a blind eye toward the escapes that went on almost daily, and they were known to accept bribes to look the other way and allow prisoners to get through. Like most of the people who were still alive after a couple of years in the camps, my mother, my sister, and I wanted to get out as quickly as possible. My grandfather gave us that chance."

"My father's father and mother were still in Kruschiwl. They were lucky because they were allowed to stay in their own home, even though other people were living with them. My Grandfather Mathias was a *Gutscher,* one of the men who transported goods from town to town. He was able to scrounge up food and other things this way. He got by by selling goods he kept hidden, item by item. One of the last things he sold to the partisans was a horse harness. This horse harness brought in enough money to buy him and his wife passage on a freight train that took them all the way to Austria. There was even enough left over so that my mother could use it to bribe our way out of the camp in Kruschiwl."

"We went to Hungary first. In Hungary, it was strange. Everything was fine there; Germans were still living peacefully there at home as if the war and the occupation in Yugoslavia had never happened."

"We stayed in two towns in Hungary. First we went to a place called Gara and stayed with the Knipp family. The Knipps were relations on my mother's side. In Gara I learned how to milk cows. Through word of mouth, I got a job as a live-in maid to German families. It paid very little, but it gave me room and board. I had to work three months for a pair of shoes. My mother sewed for people in their homes and was able to make extra money."

"It wasn't long before the communists came to Gara and expelled the Germans there. At least they didn't put them in camps like they did to use in Kruschiwl. They just arrived one day with trucks and put everyone's belongings on them and transported them out. Those Germans went on to Germany and many did well there. The Knipps ended up in Germany, and to this day, own a successful leather purse and wallet factory."

"After about a year in Gara, my mother, sister, and I decided to go to Waschgut, Hungary, where my mother's mother is from. My mother's sister-in-law lived there and so we went to stay with her for another two months."

"People were coming home from Russia then and word arrived that my father and other friends were already in Salzburg, Austria, so we made the decision to go there. I remember leaving Waschgut in a truck, and I know we paid people to transport us. They took us near the Austrian border at night—we were always crossing borders at night—and then we had to walk through the dark woods for a long time. A guide took us through the woods and we walked along with our bundles of things, moving them along, and when they got too heavy, we would stop and rest. It seemed like forever. Picking up our bundles and moving them a few feet, and then going back to pick up the rest and move them ahead to our new piles. Over and over again. Getting up, going back, and bringing everything together again, and then farther along. Over and over again. I thought it would never end."

"Once we got close—the guide knew when the border guards were not visible—we quietly crossed the border in Fierstenfeld, Austria. In Fierstenfeld was the first refugee camp we went to where we could take a shower and really get clean. We had to move from camp to camp, from the English zone to the American zone, until we finally got to Salzburg where we wanted to be."

"The day we left for Salzburg, we went to a train station. We needed identification and we didn't have any, so we had to keep moving from car to car on our way to Salzburg. Somehow we made it OK."

"When we got to Salzburg, we couldn't get to my father right away; he lived in another refugee camp and worked in a brewery. It took us another month or two before we were able to find room at a camp that would take all of us together, including my father and his parents."

A Horse Harness Buys Freedom to Live in an Old Horse Barn

"In the beginning, my mother, sister, and I lived in a refugee camp, in one large room of an old barracks that had once been home to German soldiers and their horses. We shared that one room with another family consisting of the father, mother, and two daughters. One daughter was single and the other was married and had a husband and a child. The ten of us shared that space in that little room and we slept in bunk beds. We even shared the bunk beds. I shared my bed with the unmarried daughter and my sister and my mother shared another single bed."

"It was so hard to find housing and apartments of any kind. So, we stayed in refugee camps and found work to survive. We lived in two refugee camps: the Durchgangslager and the Rossiten Kasserne. Like I said, these were old soldier barracks and horse barns and we were crowded in there with refugees from all over Europe, who like us, were homeless and needed a place to work and to sleep."

"I was able to find work in a kibbutz. I worked as a cook for eight months, making noodles for the soup. I made an awful lot of soup there. Meat was cured there, too, kosher style. They laid it on a wooden block to let the salt soak in. This meat was also put in the soup. It was 1947 then, and like us, the Jews that lived in the kibbutz went to work by day and came to the kibbutz at night to eat and to sleep. They had been in camps, too."

"My sister, Kathy, who was 15 years old at the time, worked as a baby-sitter and nanny to German and Jewish couples. Her love for working with children developed at a very young age and she still does baby-sitting to this day."

"My grandfather, Mathias, found work as a money exchanger in Austria. Whether or not he was active on the black market, I'm not sure, but I wouldn't be surprised. All I know is he made money dealing in English pounds, American dollars, and German marks. He always was a wheeler-dealer of sorts and could get along anywhere."

"After eight months in the kibbutz, I got a job at an iron foundry called Oberrascher. I worked there first, then my sister came, and finally my father got hired. In Austria, my mother bought a sewing machine and once again took on sewing to make extra money."

"In Oberrascher, I was responsible for calibrating weights on scales before they were shipped out. We stayed there until August of 1951, when we decided to go to America. We had been in Salzburg, Austria from December of 1947, when I had just turned 19 years old, until August of 1951 when I was 22 years old."

"We were encouraged to take advantage of an immigration program and we applied and were accepted. The NCWC (National Catholic World Conference) coordinated our immigration and helped us find sponsors."

"We were on the move again. Packing was not a problem because we didn't have much. Even though we all worked in Austria, we didn't have much to show for it—a few pieces of clothing, some food. The biggest piece of luggage was mother's sewing machine."

"Shortly before leaving Austria, we began studying English in language school in Austria. My father had lived in America as a boy, so he had an idea that it would be a good move and we would be able to do all right. And, he already had some grasp of the language. So, we were encouraged and hopeful when we began our journey to America."

"I left no boyfriends behind. I had a secret admirer, though. One time someone sent me a note at the kibbutz, asking me to meet him at a certain time and place. I never went, though. I chose not to get involved with anyone because I never felt settled. I never knew when things would change again. Every so often, I still wonder who my secret admirer was."

"This is what my sister, Kathy, says about our time in Austria."

"I think that the time we spent in Austria was the happiest time for my mother. We didn't have much and we all had to rely on each other. You can get lost in acquiring things, and when things are too good, maybe you forget. My father used to say, 'If we ever get out of this camp and get enough food, we are going to eat whatever there is.' And, when we got to America, soon everybody went on a diet. You can't have this. You can't have that. Sometimes you forget the promises you made. I would never do that."

"The best memories I have of Austria are the friendships I shared with other people in the same situation. Salzburg was a beautiful city. We had a wonderful time, there. We walked it from one end to the other. We went to dances, to movies, and to the theater. We just needed a little bit of money. We didn't have much clothing. My mother sewed a lot. She took old clothes apart and sewed us new ones."

Coming to America

"Our journey began by train from Salzburg to Bremerhaven, Germany, where we got on a boat called the General Taylor. The General Taylor was an army boat that took soldiers to Korea and picked up immigrants in Germany on its way back to the United States."

"I was so sea sick on that boat. It was the longest time of my entire life, even though it was probably only ten days. I was supposed to work on the boat serving food, which I did the first night we set sail. But by the next morning when I woke up and we were already out on the open sea, I couldn't pick up my head anymore. That was the end of that for the next week. It took me until I was almost 65 years old until I would get on a boat again. I went on a cruise on the Big Red Boat with my son and his family."

"When we arrived at Ellis Island, I knew the boat was going to dock and I stood on deck watching it pull into New York Harbor. The Statue of Liberty was holding her arms wide to me and I was excited with anticipation. I didn't know where we were going next. I didn't know who our sponsors were going to be yet. And, because we pulled in on Labor Day—a holiday—I had to stay on the boat for one more night before I could find out."

Back to the Barracks

"The next morning all the sponsors came to pick up the immigrants. This is how it worked. You waited until your name was called and then you found out who had picked you. When our turn came we were put on a train to go to a canning factory at Seabrook Farms in New Jersey. At Seabrook Farms, they put us in a barracks again, but this was a large one where there was a lot of room."

"We canned vegetables from the fall harvest for about two and a half months. winter was just around the corner and we knew we would have to go to find other work. We soon received word from Chicago. The Jungs, people originally from our town, were already there and they told us to come. We agreed, and then went to Philadelphia to board a Greyhound bus to Chicago."

Chicago Winter, 1951

"We lived in several apartments when we got to Chicago. Housing was very difficult to come by. When we first arrived, Mrs. Faltum, a family friend that lived on south Dorchester, gave us a bedroom for a few days. Then we went on to stay with the Jungs for awhile on 47th Street. Finally, we got word from Mr. Rendel, another family friend who was a building janitor in the Lake Park area, that a studio apartment was available. We moved into our first apartment."

"This studio apartment had a Murphy bed, which my parents slept in. My sister and I slept on a pullout couch. There was a table there during the day that we moved out of the way at night so we could all sleep."

"We all worked at the same places in Chicago. The first place we worked was at an auto lamp factory. Then, for better wages, we moved on to the Revere Camera Company, where I wired tape recorders. Soon we were able to save enough money to buy a used car so we would have an easier time going to and coming from work. It was cold in winter and we had to make several transfers on the bus, so the car really came in handy."

"We didn't stay long at the studio apartment—maybe a year—and then we moved to a one-bedroom apartment on 47th Street where Mr. Jung was a janitor. My father eventually got a job as a building janitor at 1616 E. 69th Street and then we all moved there to a one-bedroom apartment. The rest of us stayed on at the Revere Camera Company and I worked there until I got married in June of 1953. Eventually my sister left to study to become a beautician."

"My sister listened to country western music and read True Stories. Somehow she was able to follow the stories. She loved to read. My sister and I went to the Lincoln Turner Hall on the north side in the German neighborhood where they had dances. Most of our people went there to dance and meet each other. These functions made it easier to leave Austria behind. We also went to a German movie theater on Southport. We took the El everywhere at night. It was cheap transportation and very safe back then. We had a lot of fun going out."

"I met my husband, Henry, at a German dance at Lincoln Turner Hall. Henry was from the Romanian Banat, from a Danube Swabian farming village just like the one I had been raised in. He was one year older than me, so he had been sent at 16 to work in Russia. He spent four years there. When he was released, he went to Germany for a short time before coming to America."

"Like other immigrants, I learned to speak English by taking classes at Englewood High School at night. Henry, who lived on the north side with his aunt and uncle, was a machinist apprentice and was taking English classes at Schurz High School."

"My family and I liked everything in America when we came here. It was a new place—a new start—and there was lots of opportunity. Everybody had work and everybody got someplace. We were all hardworking people and we made a go of it."

"The very nice part, we always said, was that people were so helpful to us. They were used to all kinds of people coming to America. When you went for a job, they were helping you with every word you wanted to say. People were always helpful. They couldn't do enough for us. They helped us fill out our work applications and showed us what to do."

◆   ◆   ◆

There is a reluctance on the part of immigrants—especially those who have survived ethnic cleansing and slave labor of the concentration camps—to totally assimilate. In oh so many everyday and seemingly invisible ways, their lives take on the heartbeat of the reconstructionist: refashioning and reinventing themselves in a new environment, yet not with a completely clean slate.

From the chalk dust of virtual erasure, they leave their footprints everywhere. Look closely and you can see them clogging the checkout lines of discount grocery stores, carefully checking the items on their sales receipts, in the pews of churches, hands pressed devoutly to their faces in prayer, on the wooden dance floors at their summer picnics, a good-toothed smile flashes over a shoulder, and upon the foreheads and psyches of their children, like me, who grow up proudly, and yes, a bit schizophrenically, navigating the duality of their European-American households.

I was expected to speak German at home, to save instead of spend, to learn the cooking and cleaning skills of a good *Hausfrau*, to eat when I wasn't hungry—so as not to offend a loving hostess—to be smart enough to defer to men in public, and to marry a German boy because 'we would understand each other better.' Instead, I leaned more to my American side; I preferred the life of a rebel.

I spoke English whenever I could and chastised my parents when they hid behind their German tongues. I spent a lot of time in my room reading, instead of in the kitchen peeling carrots. I developed a weight problem that had me alternating between every diet known to man that was water-, protein-, or carbohydrate-based, and apologizing to the baffled faces of several well-meaning, yet oblivious women, holding creme slices and apricot cookies under my nose. I gravitated toward feminism and learned to resent my brother for having the luxury of being able to act out on occasion and for having the good fortune to be born a boy, which in our home meant guaranteed seating on the upside of a double standard. Throughout high school, and much to my mother's dismay, I dated Mexicans, Italians, Swedes, and Poles. German boys didn't stand a chance. But, I did enjoy going to the bank. One out of six isn't all that bad.

◆   ◆   ◆

As eastern European minority Germans, my parents endured a bumpy ride of rapidly changing landscapes and diverse identities: from farmers to slaves to refugees to displaced persons to immigrants. And, like Adam, God touched them by their fingertips and through the blessed sweat of their brows, they were able to recreate themselves out of the rubble.

They learned to laugh again.

"Who are you? Where did you come from?"

I'm forever asking people those questions.

"We're DP's," they would giggle in reply, my father's lips pulled wide in a smile that revealed his big square teeth. My mother would smile knowingly in return. Yes, the DPs had made out just fine.

They became landowners again. Their waving rows of wheat, corn, and barley were transformed into vertical columns of apartment buildings, in which they nurtured the seeds of many lives just beginning in neat, one-bedroom apartments.

"We're running a honeymoon house," my father would joke and complain because the tenants never stayed more than a year or two before moving on to start families of their own.

My parents had their first apartment building before I was even born, and they kept it until I was a freshman in college. My mother's parents owned a large 13-flat on the corner of Byron and Ridgeway, also on Chicago's northwest side, that was directly across the street and almost as large as my high school. I had lunch there occasionally with my grandmother and she would complain that the students littered her vestibules with cigarette butts. That immense red brick apartment building was on a double lot; it had two vestibules that served three floors of apartments each. Every Monday morning my grandmother cleaned them and the hallways that rose up behind the heavy glass doors, vacuuming the carpeted stairs and shining up the balustrades.

All of the men in my family, with the exception of my Uncle Jakob, were janitors of apartment buildings, either someone else's or their own. My Uncle Adam was the onsite maintenance engineer at 3450 N. Sheridan Road until he retired 30 years later. My Uncle Peter was his bookend to the south: an onsite janitor in a south Shore high-rise for about as many years.

Being a janitor was the perfect job for the men when they first set foot in this country. First of all, they were skilled in manual labor. They were adept mechanically, and they had a natural affinity for carpentry, machinery, and landscaping. They already knew how to cultivate farmland, and had learned how to build barns and repair threshing machines. Those skills could easily be converted into building maintenance on a one-half acre city lot.

Secondly, they could work independently as they learned the language. It was not necessary to carry on lengthy conversations with tenants as they carefully edged the lawns in summer and adjusted the boiler heat on frigid Chicago winter nights. Most importantly, perhaps, as resident janitors, they got guaranteed housing. An apartment in the building was included in the salary. And that's exactly what they needed in the beginning, in a city in which housing was scarce—a place for their families to live and a job close to home because many hadn't yet accumulated savings to buy a car.

It was a perfect job to which they were ideally suited. In fact, it became their ticket to front-row seating. With the money they saved on rent, they were soon able to use to buy their own apartment buildings and their own homes.

The women and the men worked side by side in the care of their property. I watched my father take care of the heating, the electrical, the plumbing, and the snow and garbage removal. My mother helped with the showing and the renting, the cleaning and the painting, and the landscaping.

On Tuesdays, after we moved to our new home on Kilpatrick, my mother, brother, and I would mount our bicycles and ride over to the apartment building on Kildare. We rambled through the side streets, my other out in front, leading her goslings, I on my blue and white bike with the banana handle bars and my brother coming up the rear on his little red bike. Once there, 45 minutes later, my mother got to work cutting the grass and tidying up the hallways while my brother and I played in the yard, picking cherries in the summer and apples in the fall from the fruit trees that grew there. We'd bundle the cherries up in an old plastic bag, tie them on the handlebars and ride them home in the afternoon. Later on my mother used them to make the most delicious, sugar-sprinkled cherry slices.

They worked like I don't know how. And, they actually liked it. It was always a big project when a tenant moved out and they had to ready the apartment for the next one coming in. The apartments had to be thoroughly cleaned, from top to bottom, freezers defrosted and ovens sprayed with Easy Off, charred pizza remains wiped into a rag. Walls were painted and wallpapered in record time. In their heyday, my mother and grandmother would team up and transform an apartment in a day and a half. It was something to see. The two of them poring over wallpaper remnants that my grandmother would pull down from the top shelf of her storage closet. Was there something here that could still be put to good use? In the stifling heat of August when no one had any air conditioners yet, I would watch fat beads of sweat run in rivulets from the kerchiefs tied around their foreheads, while tiny beads popped up on their upper lips. Their faces and upper arms flushed pink as they rolled out the ceilings in white. Always in perfect white.

"It makes the room look bigger," my mother used to say.

Resourceful, tenacious, hardworking, proud, practical, responsible people. They had taken a tumultuous journey and had come full circle: from haves to have-nots to haves again. They had come close to being eradicated; they had recreated themselves; they were lords of their manor once again. And their expectations ran high. The shadow they cast was sometimes too great to bear.

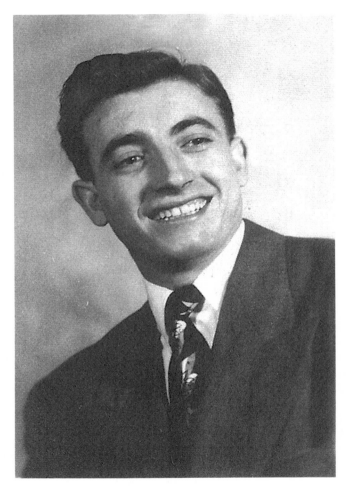

Henry Andor as a young immigrant.

"For my mother, it was bread. For my father, it was being educated."

"What's this *B* doing on your report card?"

It is mid-semester of my eighth grade and my father is scanning the five grades, four of which are *A*'s, and he has locked on the *B* with a disapproving note to his voice.

"It's Math, Dad," I stammer. I just can't get those word problems in Algebra."

English is not my father's subject, but Math is. As a tool and die maker, he can decipher specifications at a glance and knows when a blueprint can be mechanically produced. As a carpenter, he knows the geometry of angles and areas just fine. And, I'll be darned if I know how, with a sixth-grade education, he can figure out how fast two trains are going when they finally meet at their East-west intersection point.

He squints at me from behind his square-shaped, wire-framed glasses, reaches in his pocket for the four dollars (he pays $1 for each *A*), and agrees to spend some time after dinner with me on rate, time, and distance problems.

◆　　　◆　　　◆

When I think of him now, I think the word *precision*. My father did everything with precision. The way he walked, at a crisp, swift clip; the way he stood, shoulders squared, back straight; the way he danced, chest impenetrable, while legs glided light and free as an ice skater; and the way he worked, to the quarter of a millimeter and never a hair off.

He even had a precise way of sprinkling the lawn. Standing tall with the hose in his right hand, a Raleigh cigarette clamped in his teeth, he carefully outlined the grass, edges first as if he were drawing a picture, careful not to water the sidewalk. Around the square he'd go, and then like a magician, he'd wave his wand back and forth, back and forth, the water drops gracefully falling in a beautiful arc as he colored in the lines.

He wore sleeveless tee-shirts on a hairless chest, stuffed neatly into baggy dark brown or gray chinos. Actually, he had three hairs on his chest. One day I spied him in the reflection of his bedroom mirror, he head bent down, pulling each one out with my a pair of my mother's tweezers. He never wore jeans; denim felt too confining for him. He liked his pants loose and his shirts on the formfitting side. He had dark brown hair, which he combed straight back, a strong forehead over heavy dark eyebrows, and a good-sized, yet tapered patrician nose. He had a beautiful smile. His lips pulled wide to show his strong squared teeth, and his whole face would light up, brown eyes twinkling. He was a handsome, broad-shouldered man, my father, a regular Danube Swabian James Dean.

◆   ◆   ◆

In the 23 years I knew my father, I saw him cry four times. The first time it happened, I was still in grade school, probably in sixth or seventh grade. I remember him standing beside me, on my left, in the pew in St. Edward's Church. He rarely went to church; that was something that my brother and I did with my mother. We had come to the part in the service where the priest invokes mercy on the souls of the recently departed. The priest calls out a chosen few by name, usually those whose relatives have purchased masses in which they are to be honorably mentioned, and then finishes up with the *"and all those who have recently departed,"* or something like that, if my memory serves me correctly. The priest called out the name of my father's mother, and suddenly his rigid body shuddered, jerking almost imperceptibly in place, and I felt the power of the self-control he had to summon to prevent him from breaking into tears. He shifted a few times and I tried not to notice his discomfort. But I glanced over anyway, looking for the tears I might see glistening on his cheek. He was like an open door in the moments before a rainstorm; the changing wind kept blowing him open and closed, open and closed, until the latch clicked tightly shut.

He'd just received word a day or two before that she had died. News came so sporadically and reluctantly out of Romania in the late 60's; he didn't even have time to get a plane ticket. She was already dead and buried and he couldn't do a thing about it except wait for the photo of her in the casket that would arrive by mail, and come to this foreign place to hear a stranger say her name.

He'd tried all during his years as an immigrant in America to get his parents out of Romania. They were elderly people who had once had a small farm and they had no other skills to offer their country. But, still, the Romanian authorities would not let them go.

My father's sister, Cilli (short for Cecilia), and her husband, Rafael, a civil engineer, were in similar straits; they were prisoners of a country from which they had always tried to conspire with my father their escape. Once Cilli wanted him to buy them a car. This way, she reasoned, they could receive permission to go on a car trip out of the country. Cilli's plan for defection went like this: they would take the care and go on the vacation and return at the specified time. They would do it again, same way, no changes, the next year. And, finally, the third time, after they had established a level of trust with the Romanian authorities, they would leave as they had always done, with a few suitcases packed and everything else left behind in the apartment, and they would never return. It was a clever plan, my father conceded, but there were two problems he foresaw in the scenario which caused him to refuse her: he had to buy her a car, and once she and Rafael and their son Rafi, Jr. sped away to freedom, there would be no one left in Romania to watch over his parents.

The first and only time I ever met my father's mother was when I was ten years old and my family was on the Romanian leg of our *Roots* trip. We had just driven in and out of what was left of my mother's town of Kruschiwl, Yugoslavia, and we were now off to spend two weeks in my father's town of Benschekul de Sus, Romania.

What I remember of Romania is this: The big, brown staring eyes of the townspeople looking at us arrive in the dusty, white Opel Kadett. Reddish-brown clay dirt roads, a gaggle of geese sharing my path, and a woman in heavy dark skirts and babushka who must have been all of 35 years old with missing front teeth. A star and sickle on a dusty, red stone monument in the center of town. What I remember of my father's mother is this: A small woman with a wizened face, peering out of the blackness of a heavy, black babushka and a long, pin-striped apron covering a heavy black skirt.

The night we arrived in Benschek, she wanted to make our first family dinner a memorable experience. She selected the rooster to slaughter, an honor bestowed on only the finest of guests. I can see her in the backyard, black skirt hooked wide, the whiteness of the rooster's feathers twirling in her gnarled hands, the redness of the blood ringing his headless collar as he strutted sporadically about the dusty yard, and the way she looked at my startled face and laughed. Later I smelled the rooster blood and onions cooking in a skillet on the stove; it was heavy and dark and had a strong odor like burning dirt. The rooster did not taste like a chicken I had ever eaten before. The meat was hard and full of muscle and gristle. I dutifully ate it and then went out to the porch with my father's sister, Cilli, and we threw it all up.

One day my grandmother tried to teach my brother how to slaughter a rabbit. She reached into the rabbit hutch, the furry creatures scurrying to avoid the clutching grasp of her hand. She pulled one unlucky fellow out and held him up by the hind legs. She motioned to my eight-year-old brother, showing him where to make his karate chop in the rabbit's neck. My brother made a few unsuccessful attempts to knock the rabbit out. Then she showed him the right way. One well-placed chop, the body flung sideways on an old tree stump, and furry rabbit head falling, sliding away from a glistening silver blade in one, clean slice. I turned away. That night was the first and last time I ever ate rabbit.

On the farm they had a well, and I remember looking into the hole, watching her pull the rope hand over hand to finally reveal a bucket which contained butter, cheese, a piece of smoked ham, and milk. (This, I presumed, was the refrigerator.) Coming from the land of McDonald's and Pizza Hut, I had a hard time comprehending that this was where my father grew up, in this little dusty town in what was left of the Romanian Banat.

Ethnic Germans, like those on my mother's side, had also settled farther east along the Danube Basin to farm in Romania. But, unlike my mother's family in Yugoslavia, they were allowed to stay in Benschek. And, that completes the equation; I am ethnic German—one-half Yugoslavian Batschka on my mother's side and one-half Romanian Banat on my father's side. The biggest difference between the two groups, as far as I have been able to discern, is that my mother's ethnic dress was not as dark as the Romanians' and the Batschka men did not wear the ribboned and decorated hats in the Kirchweih festival procession like the men do in Romania. Otherwise, they're cut out of the same cloth.

Little did I know when I said good-bye to my father's mother, clutched tightly to her black bosom two weeks later, that it would be the last time I would ever see her again.

◆   ◆   ◆

The second time I saw my father cry, we were at the funeral service of Tante Becker. Tante Becker (we called her *Tunda)* was my father's aunt, and she had been living in America long before the Second World War. She had come to the U.S. as a young aupere girl of 13 with her girlfriend, whom I knew as Mrs. Zimmerman. *Tunda* married Peter Becker, also from Benschek, who at the time used to deliver Butternut and Roman Meal bread to homes in Chicago by horse and buggy. Up until I was four-and-a-half years old, we lived about a block away from Aunt and Uncle Becker in a beautiful, red brick and graystone in which is now the Old Irving Park area, just down the block from the YMCA at 3913 N. Kildare Avenue.

Then, like the first time he cried, I sat beside my father, to his right, this time in the nursing home where the funeral service was being held. It was February of 1979 and I was 23 years old. Mrs. Zimmerman's son, Albert, was giving the eulogy. Albert got to the part in the eulogy where he was recounting all the special incidents in *Tunda's* life when she made a difference in other people's lives. Soon enough the subject of father came up.

"I remember when *Tunda* saw her nephew, Henry, for the first time," Albert recalled. "The Beckers were all there at O'Hare Field waiting for the passengers on Henry's plane to disembark. They were nervous and excited because they hadn't seen Henry before and weren't sure what he was going to look like. Then, all of a sudden, *Tunda's* son, Walter shouted out, 'Look. That's him. That's Henry. See, he's wearing my old coat.'"

This is the part in the eulogy where my father's door on its rusty hinges started flapping open. He had to fight so hard to pull it shut again, but this time a strangled sob escaped his lips.

Uncle and Tante Becker were my father's immigration sponsors, and on that night in 1949, they were able to recognize his scrawny, windblown head poking out of Walter's old hand-me-down coat that was probably *oohed* and *aahed* about as my father's long fingers once carefully pulled it out of a much-needed care package. While listening to the eulogy, I learned that Tante Becker had welcomed my father as another grown-up son into her home, and had given him the first roof over his head and had shared the first of many meals in the United States of America with him. They opened their door and their hearts to him and it was Tante Becker with her hand on the doorknob, holding it out wide.

While he lived in the in-law apartment they had on the second floor of their white Victorian farmhouse with the expansive front porch I so admired, he apprenticed himself as a tool and die maker, a job he held until the day he died 30 years later. I remember him telling me once that in the world of work he had two choices. When he came to America, he knew a man named Mr. Schicht who owned a grocery store, and he could have become a produce manager. But, he chose to be a machinist instead.

When he married my mother a couple of years later, they lived in his upstairs apartment until they could afford to buy the red brick and graystone apartment building just two years later. When they moved in in 1955, my mother was pregnant with me. My mother told me he cried sometimes at night in bed with her, laying his head on her round belly, wondering aloud to my unborn ears, how, on earth, he was ever going to manage fatherhood and his mortgage at the same time.

◆   ◆   ◆

I sat beside my father on his right in the car, too, during those times when my brother didn't get his turn in the front passenger seat. I gazed out the window of a white Chevrolet Impala that turned into a green Pontiac Catalina, but still we traveled the same streets. My father loved his modest ranch home, and even when all of his friends started moving to the suburbs, he dug his heels into the northwest side of Chicago for the long haul.

On our outings to the bank, we drove down Cicero Avenue to Irving Park Road and then made a right turn. We pulled into the busy parking lot of the Irving Federal Savings in the days before direct deposit, in the days before it became Tallman Home Savings, in the days before it became LaSalle Bank, and stood in long lines that snaked throughout the entire lobby. It took forever to get to the teller; it was like twisting and turning and waiting to get on the latest ride at Riverview—an amusement park that has since turned into a shopping center. When we finally made it to the teller, I was the one who shoved the checks and deposit slips over the counter, reaching up less and less over the years.

From the time I was about five years old, I already had a savings account. I don't remember opening it; I just know I had my own passbook. Whenever there was a holiday celebration, the passbook would appear. Relatives always gave monetary gifts, so five dollars from each family easily turned into $25 or more.

It usually went like this. My brother and I would be watching TV—*Speedracer* or *All-Star Wrestling* on a Saturday morning and my father would come into the living room with his paycheck in hand.

"How much gift money did you get?" he'd ask.

"Five dollars from Oma and Ota, $5 from Aunt Sali and Uncle Adam, $5 from Aunt Eva and Uncle Jakob, $5 from Aunt Kathy, $5 from Uncle Peter and Aunt Mary, and $2 from Great Grandmother and Great Grandfather Thoebert."

He'd screw up his face a little and smile when I'd get to the $2.

"OK, that's—"

"Twenty-seven dollars," I'd pipe in.

"Ja. $27."

Then he'd ask *the question*.

"How much do you want to keep and how much do you want to put in the bank?"

I already knew my deposit had to be greater than my cash back. My father had already taught me the simple equation of saving money: you had to keep more than you spent. It wasn't how much you made; in the end, it only mattered what you had left.

I'd think about Reese's peanut butter cups and Snicker's bars and penny candy I could get at the corner store.

"I'll keep $5," I said, thinking that would keep me in candy for a long time.

"OK. That leaves $22 for your bank account."

He'd turn to my brother who was sprawled out on his belly in his pajamas on the floor.

"What about you, Henry. How much do you want to save?"

"Twenty-seven dollars," he'd reply, without skipping at beat.

We'd sign our checks and organize our cash into envelopes and sometimes I'd accompany my Dad to the bank. Speedracer and All-Star Wrestling were not my favorite TV shows.

A day or two later I'd catch my brother borrowing $5 from my father, who never asked for it back. My brother got a head start in grasping the concept of using other people's money a lot earlier than I did. At the time, I just thought he was cheap.

◆   ◆   ◆

My parents belonged to the Danube Swabian Club. This club was a group of ethnic Germans like themselves that had emigrated to the Chicago area and gathered together to celebrate, commemorate, and preserve their cultural heritage. The Danube Swabian Club primarily hosted dinner dances at special times of the year: Christmas and New Year's Eve parties, Easter and Mother's Day in the spring, and Schlachtfest (slaughter feast), which was held in the fall to commemorate the annual slaughter of the family pig.

I scurried around Lincoln Turner Hall with my girlfriend Kathy Meister in our taffeta party dresses with drink tickets clutched in our sticky hands. That is, until my mother caught ahold of me and roughly wiped Schwarzwaelder Kirsch Torte (Black Forest Cherry Cake) off my face with a crumpled up napkin. I happily stood on my father's shoes, stretching my hands up to him, as he taught me how to waltz on the dance floor. I carefully recited a poem in German for Mother's Day, and got to wear a sparkly hat and toot a paper horn at midnight at my first New Year's Eve party.

When I was in 4th grade, the Danube Swabian Club organized a German School for the children like myself, whom they felt could benefit from language and history studies. They employed a teacher named Herr Schmidt to do the job. We started school at the Lincoln Turner Hall and, after about a year, we moved to St. Alphonsus School on Southport.

I hated Saturday mornings when my father would drive my brother and me to German School. Instead of getting to play Barbies and Monopoly with my friend Janice Bilder who lived two doors away, I had to go to school six days a week.

During class at German School, I went through another upsetting experience. I lived through the humiliation of raising my hand and always giving the wrong answers to Herr Schmidt's questions.

"What is the word for *hair,*" he'd ask.

"Ja," he'd reply to my waving arm.

"*Hor,*" I'd confidently announce.

"Nein," he'd quickly reply.

That's what my parents always used to say. I wrinkled my brow in confusion.

"The word is *haare* (pronounced ha-ray)."

Then he went on to the next one.

"Das wort fuer *have,* bitte."

My hand shot up again. Eager to redeem myself, I blurted out, *hab.*

"Nein," he corrected me again. "The word is *habe* (pronounced ha-bay)."

I learned that I was speaking in the chopped slang endings of Schwaebisch, the German dialect my father and mother had taught me. Herr Schmidt was teaching high German, a language I did not know. To this day, I am always a little embarrassed and self-conscious when I try to speak in German.

During the years of German School, fourth through eighth grade, my father on occasion would attempt to complement my studies by imposing culture law on me.

"There will be no talking at the dinner table unless it is in German," he'd announce and reach over for a piece of bread to soak up the goulash gravy on his plate.

My brother and I would just look at each other, roll our eyes and settle in to notice how loudly silver wear can scrape on a plate. We did not flinch; our father never received a sparkling repartee of our day's activities in high, flawless German. Instead, we epitomized another favorite childhood adage. We were seen, albeit with stubbornly clenched jaws, but we were not heard. Somewhere along the line, my father gave it up.

He was doing the same thing with us that he did with the notepad he kept by the telephone. Over and over again in his beautiful handwriting he'd write his name and the place of his birth: Henry Andor, Benschekul de Sus, Romania. He'd fill an entire note page. It was as if he were a prisoner of war and he could only reply when asked a question with his name, rank, and serial number. Over and over again, he reaffirmed his identity to himself, and in his own way, he tried to make us understand who he was and what he was all about. My mother and father belonged to a minority subculture of Germans who had been stripped of their identities and were lucky enough to survive to recreate them. At the time, I just didn't understand and couldn't have—even if he'd tried to explain it to me.

◆   ◆   ◆

When he did try to talk seriously to me once, I didn't listen. I was watching television, so I wasn't completely focused on what he was saying. In retrospect, I wish I had been paying better attention to him because it was the only time my father ever shared any of his fears with me. He was always trying to be so strong; that night he was a reluctant Atlas with the weight of the world pressing down upon his shoulders. It is one of my greatest regrets that I did not listen more closely to him that night.

My father was telling me that my parents were finally going to sell their apartment building—the one they'd kept in Old Irving Park, even after we had moved into the ranch home on Kilpatrick that my father loved so when I was about 4-1/2 years old. Through the laugh track of the sitcom, I heard his voice telling me that he was ready to get out of the landlord business. He'd had his fill of shoveling snow in the morning before he started his machinist job—first at his house, then at the building. And, he wasn't going to miss running off in the evenings when he was tired from his day making molds to let some tenant in the apartment who had locked himself out. But my mother and her parents had other ideas.

My mother's parents had just sold their 13-flat apartment building in Chicago and were eyeing another nine-flat in Harwood Heights. They wanted my mother and father to go along with them on the deal to buy the new apartment building. It was important to them that their money be reinvested promptly, so as to avoid paying unnecessary capital gains taxes.

That night, while I was home on break from college, my father's tired voice tried to reach out to me woefully from the beige sofa near the picture window where he sat.

"Ingrid, I really don't want to do it. I'm tired. I just want to do my job and come home. I'm not going to live to be an old man."

He said that a lot over the years.

I'm not going to live to be an old man.

I turned away from the silly sitcom that competed for his attention and offered him this crumb.

"Then don't do it. You don't want to do it, and you know what makes you happy, so just don't do it."

I turned back to the TV without realizing what he was crying about. It was three against one, he was up against the wall, and he wasn't going to make it.

Not six months after the deal went through, my grandfather suffered a stroke, which painfully paralyzed his right hand, and my father was stuck shoveling snow again at a much bigger building. He did it for almost three more years until his prophesy came true. He died a young man, like he always knew he would, at the age of 52, on Christmas Day in 1979. My grandfather, in shock, followed him one week later on January 5th, and my grandmother honored my father's memory by dying fours years later on Christmas Day, 1983. Eighteen years have gone by and my mother is now just beginning to consider putting that building up for sale. For the sake of his memory, I hope she does it soon.

◆   ◆   ◆

My mother told me about another time my father cried. A time when I was not beside him. She said he cried on the way home from dropping me off at my new dorm room at the University of Illinois during New Student Week of my freshman year.

Aside from always providing a roof over my head, which always included an expansive bedroom for me—something I must have even to this day—he was adamant about providing for a good college education.

"Ingrid," he used to say, "they can take everything away from you, except what's in here."

He'd point knowingly to his temple, opening his brown eyes wide and jutting that long squared machinist's index finger.

For my mother, it was bread. For my father, it was being educated. From the time my brother and I were little children, the savings plans were already in place so that a college education would always loom before us.

My parents never went to high school or college, so they didn't know what form of study I should pursue. My father thought I had a way with words. I could write papers and make speeches pretty well, and he thought those skills would bring me success as a lawyer. Both of my parents agreed that college would also make me a more attractive mate for an educated man. They absolutely insisted on college. It was never a point of discussion. I had a lot of trouble my first year trying to nail down the right major, and I came the hard way to Journalism via Business Administration three years later.

My first year at the University of Illinois was extremely challenging. Classes were difficult, and I often felt that my private high school education did not sufficiently prepare me for the type of study I was experiencing. Small, attentive high school classes did not translate well to large, impersonal lecture halls filled with hundreds of students scribbling in their notebooks.

In addition, the restriction of a double-standard upbringing by my immigrant parents was suddenly removed and I was free to float in a sea of 40,000, 18- to 25-year-olds. It was heaven—for awhile. Like many of my compatriots, I swam down current into mix of experimentation with drugs. The tide rose around me like a seiche and I eventually submerged. Frantic and fearful one night that I would not be able to complete a term paper, I broke down in the campus library, feeling like the walls of the study carrel were closing in on me. The next morning found me huddled in the corner of my dorm room, unable to rise from bed and dress for fear that the other students would see me for the failure that I was. My coming of age had happened too quickly; the threshold of my adulthood rose to trip me, and at 19 years of age, I was in the throes of a full-blown nervous breakdown.

Soon enough I was back at home, dazed and confused and staring into the disappointed face of my father. The lines of his mouth pulled downed sorrowfully, and I will never forget what he said to me one night in despair.

"I never thought your brother would make anything of himself. I thought you would be the one."

My vacant eyes watched him break down in tears and turn away, my windswept mind unable to comprehend that my teenage folly had caused him to give up on me forever. No longer would my father have any expectations—good or bad—of me.

◆   ◆   ◆

My father never talked much about the hardships he endured as a teenage boy of 16. In 1944, while my mother was working in the fields for the communist partisans in Yugoslavia, my father became another statistic in the Russian *war reparations* human cargo train. The Russians went east down the road to the Romanian Banat and helped themselves to approximately 50,000 ethnic Germans there. My father was taken to a labor camp in Siberia where he was assigned to help rebuild railroads and work in the coal mines.

One night he and a man about 40 years old decided to escape the camp. They set out but didn't get very far before the Russians and their dogs tracked them down. The commander of the camp had the man beaten up badly until he was near death. When it was my father's turn to receive the first backhanded blow with the butt of a gun, he pretended to be knocked out so the beating would stop. The commander imprisoned them both for the night and announced that they would be shot before the camp inmates the following day. I imagine him passing a fitful night, visions of a life he would never experience haunting his half-dreams.

The next day when they came for him, he experienced a miraculous reprieve. The commander suddenly changed his mind and had them moved to another camp. By moving them to the other camp, he could spare their lives and still keep the other inmates ignorant of their fate.

I think it's from the hunger he experienced in Russia that he developed the saying that he was so fond of repeating when my brother and I turned our noses up at one of my mother's dinners.

"When you're hungry, you'll eat shoe leather," he'd announce to us before turning back to his plate.

My father was in the Russian labor camp for four years until he was released. He then spent another year in Germany as a refugee before coming to America to live with Tante and Onkel Becker in the big white Victorian farmhouse.

My father did not meet my mother until after he emigrated to the United States. They met at a German dance on Lincoln Avenue at the Lincoln Turner Hall. Sometimes I wonder what their first conversation was like. Can you imagine them discussing their similar backgrounds and concentration camp experiences? No small talk, that. Somehow, in the midst of that serious conversation, they realize that they have an awful lot in common. Is it possible that they were destined to meet? Perhaps he charmingly alluded to it and saw understanding and acceptance in her soft, hazel eyes. Then he probably asked her to dance. Maybe that's where the falling in love part happened.

Like many Danube Swabian men, my father was a fabulous dancer. In my freshman year of high school, he took me to the father-daughter dance that my high school hosted and he got to show off his stuff, fox-trotting me across the fresh polish of the gym floor. I could smell the sweet sadness of the white carnation he wore in his left lapel that night as his right hand exerted a constant pressure on the small of my back, pulling me firmly upright.

"Don't move your upper body so much," he said as he glided me across the floor.

"One. Two. Three. Slide. It's all in the legs."

He was only 5'8" inches tall, but he had very broad shoulders, so he always looked tall and elegant on the dance floor.

He was on my back a lot. I never walked fast enough for him. He took short, nervous, purposeful steps, always in a hurry to do something important. I never saw him stroll. I can still hear him whispering behind my right ear.

"Faster. Faster. Take shorter steps."

He escaped death one other time when he was 12 years old. While looking up in the trees one spring day for birds' nests—his boyhood passion—he had the misfortune of stepping on a rusty nail and was soon bedridden with lock jaw. If this had happened to anyone other than my father in 1939 in Benschek—a place where no one got tetanus shots—it would most certainly have proven to be a death knell. While his mother fed him from a straw, his father got busy making a coffin for him. Maybe he scared himself well listening to the constant sawing of the wood as it interrupted his afternoon naps.

But the third time, he could not escape death. On Christmas night in 1979, after spending an uneventful day with his in-laws, his wife, his son, and me, he went home and quietly died of a massive heart attack while watching the evening news.

◆   ◆   ◆

He was not an easy man to love, but he had a presence that commanded your respect. He was a passionate man, yet he was never comfortable expressing his emotions. He was not a hugger, and I usually did not go to him to be comforted. But one night when I had trouble sleeping, he sat at the edge of my bed and rubbed perfectly concentric circles on my back with with the fingers of his strong, working man's hands.

He could build anything with his hands. The family room, the roof—they were all putty in his hands. He'd get that project look on his face—a determined spark in the captain's eyes that signaled a course for the ship was set—a pencil over his right ear, a sleeveless undershirt tucked neatly into his baggy work pants, and a cigarette clamped between his front teeth. My father liked biting the filters when he was concentrating. After a particularly creative day, I would see those chewed up filters in the ash tray, with the cotton tubing popping out of the moistened ends. One day he came home with hairy burlap strips, plastic palm fronds and coconuts, and he transformed a cement pole in the basement into a palm tree for my 14th birthday party. It became the centerpiece of a Hawaiian party I'll never forget.

He worked a lot, and except for gardening and a variety of home improvement projects, he had few personal hobbies. When my brother and I were very small children, he took us to the bowling alley with him once or twice. He had an impressive hook. Once he went fishing with our neighbor, Mr. Bilder. Like my mother, he liked to play cards. My parents belonged to a card club and each of the couples took turns hosting Saturday night card parties. They were other Danube Swabian immigrants like my parents and they played *Fuchsa* and *Mariasch* together, card games they played back home with those beautifully illustrated foreign cards that looked like they'd been painted in the Black Forest. At night, after watching the news, he liked to chew on his cigarettes and laugh with Johnny Carson. I'm glad Johnny put him to bed with a smile on his lips.

My father had a broad open smile, and he was generous with it. He was charming and well-liked, although he really didn't favor parties. It's not because he didn't enjoy the people; he just didn't like cleaning up afterwards, and he wasn't one to leave things until morning, either. He was a homebody at heart. He liked order in his house; he hated clutter. My mother was such a pack rat, it drove him insane. They were perfect for each other; he kept trying to contain her stuff. He came home from work one night and flew into a rage when he saw a stack of old newspapers about two feet high on one of the side chairs in the kitchen. He shrieked about the mess and swooped up the stack in his arms and tramped outside and threw everything in the garbage can by the alley. Was he ever surprised when it turned out that he had to buy the two library books that were hidden in the pile.

Although I have never thrown out any books *by accident*, I must say that I've inherited that same old squirrely feeling when too much junk mail and house piles start rising up against me.

◆   ◆   ◆

Shortly before he died, we had a falling out. I had worked my own way back into college, and I was in my junior year at Columbia. Even though I held down a job and had my own apartment, he did not approve of my independent lifestyle or the choices I made in friends, and he stopped talking to me. When I would go over to the house to visit my mother, he would get up stonily and remove himself from the room.

Instead of repeatedly exposing myself to the cold shoulder, I tried to tell my mother that I would prefer it if she just visited me at my apartment.

"I live here, too," she'd say, and that would be the end of it. She held her own in the stubborn department.

Now that I look back on it, I realize that I wasn't the only reason for his discomfort. He probably wasn't feeling too well physically then. His doctor had encouraged him to quit smoking because he had just been diagnosed with high blood pressure. He was nervous and edgy and impatient without his cigarettes. In addition, he was having difficulty adjusting to the blood pressure medication.

So when he died suddenly, a couple of months later, we hadn't yet gotten around to reconciling our differences. As it turned out, I was able to do it only after his death.

One night in a dream, I met him in the room where he died. He looked so good, so young, and strong. His brown eyes, which could be so fierce, were kind and open—sparkling, really. We stood face to face, toe to toe, and I told him then that I loved him and respected him and knew that I had disappointed him, but that I had to live my life according to my own choices. He seemed to understand; he wasn't fighting me. His face got soft and forgiving, and then he did what he was never able to do while he was alive. He hugged me. And that's the last memory I have of him. The light that surrounded us. The warmth of his arms around my shoulders pressing me into his chest. And his cheek pressed lightly against mine.

Henry Andor, Jr., Ingrid Andor, and Katharina Szettele Gronner.

"I remember this one fur coat they sent me.
My mother thought it was such a great coat. I hated it so much.
It was this ratty looking coat and I didn't like the feel of it,
but my mother thought it was terrific."

Eva Zettl Anile

I'm sitting here at the head of my cheap dining room table I got from Wickes with the cherry wood top and those awful black Shaker chairs I've never been happy with because they were never primed before they were painted. My cousin, Eva, sits to my right, in the really badly chipped chair, sipping a Mimosa. Kathi is across from her, pulling out photographs from her purse that show her growing up in Austria and Chicago, and Helen is sitting directly opposite from me, a little quiet and contemplative.

My cousins are settling in at my table this Sunday morning for brunch, spooning in the melon salad and slathering fresh bagels with garlic-herb and sun-dried tomato cream cheese spreads. I am popping up and down, making coffee and mimosas and checking on my eggs florentine, which I always overcook. One minute. Two minutes. Or is it 90 seconds? I never set the timer on the stove. I don't think it works anyway. A row of neon green eights has been flashing at me for months. I think I melted the knobs off the timer one night in some spirited cooking frenzy. I burned my chin the other day, too, sticking my face too close to the over door while checking on a pizza.

Back I come to the table this time with a coffee cake, and everybody gets an overdone egg in slightly browned spinach nest. Let's hope I do better with the questionnaire I've brought with me. It's got questions on it like:

"What were some of your earliest memories about growing up in Austria and Germany?"

"What do you remember about emigrating—the boat ride?"

"What was it like being a child immigrant?"

"Did the other kids call you Nazi because you could speak German?"

No one ever called me Nazi that I can remember, but with a name like Ingrid, everyone figured out sooner or later that I could speak German. When I was in the seventh grade, a boy in my class called me a German Lady Wrestler. I was German, and I was overweight, but I didn't know very much about wrestling except for the All Star Wrestling show my brother liked to watch. He might as well have called me a Nazi.

My cousins, who will begin to mark their 50th birthdays next year, are from the leading edge of the baby boomer generation. I've just skipped gaily past 40 and I'm the only one at the table that was born in America. We all have our stories.

"Remember what it was like at the kid's table?"

We laugh and reminisce about how we sat at a small card table that was set up about three feet away from the adult's table. Our parents sat at the dining room table, and to make more room we kids were served at our table. Our mothers would come one by one to bring us our plates. Once at Kathi's house we all got to sit at the card table in her room. After dinner we locked my brother out and he put up such a fit, crying and throwing himself against the door, that my father had to get up and have a talk with Helen—she was the eldest—reminding her that Henry was the only boy and we should be nicer to him. Henry was a little pest then and I don't think Helen wanted him to hear the girl talk. Years later, when Helen was home on college break with George, her fiancé, we were still all sitting at the kid's table.

Back to the questionnaire.

"What were some of your earliest childhood memories in Germany and Austria? Do you remember the friends you had? The games you played?"

Kathi is showing us the photographs she has pulled from her purse. She is all of three or four years old, posing with two smiling round-cheeked boys who flank her. The pictures were taken in the refugee camp in Graz, Austria where she spent her first five years. You can see the sides of the wooden barracks in the background of the picture.

"I always played with these boys. We used to go to a hill and go sledding. I used to think that hill was so big until I went back last summer with Kristin (her daughter) to visit my cousins, Monika and Helga. Everything looked so small. I think our sledding hill was just a snow-covered trash heap behind the camp."

Kathi laughs as we pass the pictures around.

Eva pipes in and tells us about the packages of hand-me-downs that my grand-mother would send from America.

"They used to send us old clothes. Once, they sent me this black doll. (laughter) They got it out of the garbage. (more laughter) Your grandfather was a janitor and they'd go to clean the apartments after the people left and some black people must have left the doll on the floor. I played with that doll for years until it fell apart."

"I remember this one fur coat they sent me. My mother thought it was such a great coat. I hated it so much. It was this ratty looking coat and I didn't like the feel of it, but my mother thought it was terrific."

Eva laughs really hard and asks for another Mimosa. My cousin Eva was conceived in Russia in the labor camp where her father and mother were deported. Her mother was later released to Dachau, which had been converted into apartments to house the East European refugees. Eva was born there and went to school in a newly built gas chamber that was used as a classroom. The people there told her that the gas chamber had never been used. Eva's father told me that compared to how he and his wife had been living in Russia, the two rooms they were given in this former death camp was 'paradise.'

"What was it like growing up in America?"

Kathi shows us more pictures of her taken in the apartments in Chicago where her father was employed as a maintenance engineer. Kathi was an only child, kind of like Helen, and in the pictures she is posed near that life-sized doll she had standing in the corner of her bedroom. Whenever my eyes would drift into that corner, my glance would be met by the stare of those glassy, black, unblinking eyes. No matter where I was in the room when I looked, the outcome was always the same. My head would turn away quickly, the loser again at our long-playing stare-down. *That doll was really too big.*

We all laugh about the big doll and look at more photos. There is one of Kathi at eight standing dead center with her little blond ringlets perfectly intact and the toe of her right foot pointing. A stuffed dog sits in the left corner of the frame. The picture goes from hand to hand, with humorous comments circling about its artful composition.

"Look at this. Who asked you to point your toe like that? Was it your father? I bet it was your father."

"What's with the dog? Is that just a coincidence that it just fits perfectly in the corner of the frame? Did your dad put the dog there?"

Kathi laughs and says, "I don't remember."

Here comes the picture with her mother. This is the one we all have where we wear matching mother-daughter dresses our mothers have sewed. Every hair, every fold of dress, is in place. Even so, some of us look more like our fathers anyway. There's that darn dog again this time on the right side of the frame. We all laugh. Now here comes Kathi at 12 with an accordion strapped to her chest. How she dreaded playing those duets with her father after dinner.

"How did the other children react to you in school? Did they make fun of you because you were different?

"I was ten years old in 1958 when we came over and I was put in the sixth grade, but I had to go to first grade for reading."

Eva is laughing nervously again, remembering what a big kid she was in comparison to the first graders.

"I had to stand in line with the first graders to go to the washroom."

"The teachers were worse than the kids. Some of them had absolutely no patience with kids they couldn't understand. They would talk real loud to you as if you couldn't hear."

"Did any of the other children ever call you Nazi because you could speak German?"

"Well, I was *Show and Tell* once for the eighth graders," my cousin Helen replies.

She has been a little subdued, mainly listening and letting the others talk, occasionally joining in with her early memories of coming to America on the boat. With her mother sea sick below and her father painting the boat to work off their passage, Helen at 2-1/2 was free to wander the ship. Where did she go? To the galley, of course, where they would give her bread and butter, day or night, to her heart's content. Like my mother, Helen and my other cousins list bread on their favorite foods list.

"Show and Tell? They used you for *Show and Tell?"* I ask incredulously.

As Helen begins to tell us her story, I am remembering the photo taken at my first birthday. I'm standing at a coffee table. In front of me is the birthday cake. Over my left shoulder sits Helen. Eva is beside her. We are all wearing pointy birthday hats. If I turn around at this table, we will all be in the exact same positions we were that day, our pointy hats replaced by memories, and in the place of my birthday cake, a pile of notes.

In the black and white photograph, Helen has a bemused, faraway look in her eyes, much like the one she wears today. Helen is six years old then, with spindly arms and legs and big soulful round dark brown eyes—eyes almost too big for her face, eyes as dark as coal. She has the eyes of an adult, wise beyond those of any child in her first grade class in the south Shore elementary school. She is a smart girl, something of an oddity for her classmates, being the only German immigrant in a predominately Irish-Catholic school.

"Because I could speak German, some of the older kids wanted to use me for *Show and Tell.* And the teacher let this kid take me to their class without a note from my parents or anything. When I got there, they said, 'Talk German to us. Where were you born?' And so I talked to them, and they let me go back to class. Also, when I was in the first grade, this six-year-old boy came from Germany, and I was his interpreter until he caught up."

This is a role Helen already knows and plays well. For most of her six years, she has been translating for her parents who have had difficulty in learning the language. Helen is bilingual because her parents emigrated from Austria in 1951 when she was 2-1/2 years old. As soon as she learns to speak English, she translates for her parents.

She develops a voice—her voice and theirs—and learns to communicate on their behalf to teachers, bankers, and shopkeepers. She learns to edit—to manipulate their words and other people's—an especially helpful technique at parent-teacher conferences. This is the role, the role of the interpreter and translator, that she plays for the rest of their lives. Is it any wonder that she grows up to go to college to study Journalism and become an editor later in life?

"What was it like growing up as an only child? Did it present you with any unique challenges or offer you any special benefits?"

The Helen that I know—the one that sits across from me at this table in 1997—is a not-so-only child. There was a first Helen—the Helen that my mother knew. The Helen that my mother knew—the first Helen—had big round dark eyes, too. But in the pictures, they are innocent and yielding and trusting. Helen Number 1 was a good girl, a daddy's girl, obedient to a fault. When she was 16-1/2 years old, she accompanied her father to Russia. Four months later she was dead.

The Helen that I know—Helen Number 2—was not conceived until 1949 while her parents were refugees in Austria. They conceived her in sorrow, still grieving over the loss of their first child.

"You're still young enough," the family said. "Why don't you have another child?" their friends encouraged. And so they did.

The Helen I know—Helen Number 2—was conceived in her likeness. Conceived in her honor. Conceived in her memory. And aside from their names, nothing about them is the same.

The Helen that my mother knew and the Helen that I knew were sisters that never met. The Helen that my mother knew defined the reality of the Helen that I knew. She came first and so she established what it meant to be a daughter. She's the one who took a precious piece of her mother's heart to her grave. She's the one who lined her mother's brow and creased her lips, pulling them downward into perpetual lines of sorrow, a parallel road the Helen I knew could never travel.

I wonder what it must be like to be a replacement daughter, to be born and raised under the shadow of a ghost. How can anyone compete with a deity? The dead become larger than life, impossible to know, to meet, to touch. Helen is never able to match her ghostly sister's intensity, sing to her song, or dislodge her from her final resting place, the sacred mausoleum, the cold dense granite drawer below the left ventricle of her mother's heart. The beating sound she hears in her mother's chest when she holds her and tells her that Helen Number 1 would never do this or that, she was too good, that rushing sound she hears every time her mother's heart beats—every time her heart beats—that deafening roar through which she can never hear her own voice, is Helen Number 1 laughing. And with every beat, with every accomplishment, she knows that she will never be able to compete with the magic of her memory or move the sacred altar of their love, forever like her dead sister, locked away in the crypt of their hearts.

And so she stops trying. And starts becoming herself.

Feeling groovy, Helen? You are in the 8th grade now, leading the class to Art Garfunkel and Paul Simon's hit song. *Feelin' groovy. Da-da-da da-da da-da da da-da.* You are leading one side of the class in singing, *feelin' groovy*, and the other to follow in closely, *feelin' groovy*. Helen bangs on the old wooden filing cabinets next to her desk in the back row.

She continues to bang her own drums and make her own sounds. Remember how you got your parents to buy you bongos when you agreed to attend the German club? Bang your own drum. Find your own beat.

She becomes the leader of the class in shenanigans. Instigator of the first order. Uncap your leaky fountain pen and when Sister's back is turned, chalking up a backboard, everyone follows your queue and flings the ink at Sister's starched white tunic. Fling the ink hard from the back row of the class. Watch the black liquid ink whip through the air. Leave your own mark, Helen. Cut a swath across the snow. Black. Sharp. Jagged. Raw.

In high school you attend your first Beatles concert, screaming out your new-found voice. Look up now, quickly stretch your arms high and catch Ringo's drumstick pin wheeling overhead. Stick it inside your sweater fast. Keep your secret treasure under your bed. Use it to bang on your bongos, Helen.

When you are a junior at the University of Illinois, your parents finally let you transfer down state. Freedom at last. Freedom to find your own politics. Freedom to meet your future husband. Freedom to march in the Vietnam antiwar demonstrations. Take your mother's anxious call in 1967. Reassure her that everything is fine on campus and that you are studying safe and sound in your dorm room. Now hang up that phone and get out there and march, girl, march. There are students everywhere. There is mass pandemonium. But this is real. This is cool. Be a rebel queen. Become a feminist. Graduate with honors. Edit out the sexist language from the World Book Encyclopedia. Make your own star and hitch your wagon to it. Inspire me with your indefatigably unique identity.

How did you do it? How does anyone do it? You stay free and sane because you find your own voice and keep it.

I finally speak up.

"Does anyone want another bagel? How about a Mimosa?"

◆   ◆   ◆

We look at some more pictures and laugh a little more and soon, hugged and kissed away, I am left alone clearing the table and wondering what I can say about being raised in America by European parents. My cousins, the child immigrants, and I, the first generation, all have our stories that tell the tale of growing up in two worlds—*theirs* and ours. We were Europeans at home with our parents—they more so than me—but we all still hungered to establish our American identities. We admonished our parents to speak English in front of our English-speaking friends. We bargained with them in exchange for our attendance at German School and Club. And, in a heartbeat, we traded their polkas for *I Want to Hold Your Hand*. There were friends and experiences we were always asked to leave behind. And we became adept at drifting back in and out all of the time.

My cousins came to America as children with their foreign-sounding names and funny hand-me-down clothes and toys. Depending on how old they were when they emigrated, they either had an easier or harder time of it. Like Eva, the older you are when you emigrate, the more difficult it can be until you learn the language and the culture.

My Aunt Kathy, who was 18 years old when she emigrated and still has a slight German accent, says that language skills are definitely the key.

"Once you learn the language, it gets a lot easier and better for you."

On the job. On the playground.

Once you get past the ethnic slurs, you learn there are advantages to knowing a foreign language. When you don't want to be bothered by anyone, or you want to speak privately in public, you can switch into the home lingo and people will leave you alone. Or, like my cousin, Helen, whose parents had more difficulty with the English language, you can interpret the ways of the world to your advantage—a skill everyone can benefit from. For all of us, traveling throughout the German-speaking countries of the world is a little easier. Even though Schwaebisch is a dialect German, the kind people of Munich could still point me in the direction of the bathroom at Oktoberfest.

I wonder if my cousins have ever considered living abroad again. I still fancy Switzerland as an ideal location—a land of mountains and water, blue skies, and three beautiful languages to speak on an almost daily basis. What an experience to speak French over breakfast at your favorite restaurant, Italian with your grocer, and German with the banker, all in the same day. Since my trip to San Miguel in 1997, I have also thought of living in Mexico for an extended period of time. Warm people. Warm climate. Warm food. Easy going and inexpensive. With 20 inches of snow out my window, I'm ready to sign up—*now*.

Although I appreciate being an American and the opportunities it offers me, I find the world and its people equally fascinating. It makes a lot of sense to me that I'm finishing this book in my new apartment in Albany Park—one of the most ethnically diverse neighborhoods on Chicago's northwest side. Here, too, you can speak three languages or more all in four square blocks: Korean, Thai, or Farsi at your favorite restaurant, Spanish with your neighbors, and Swedish at the gift shop.

The world is somehow smaller and less foreign when it comes to you at the dinner table every day—even if at times you squirm with the strangeness of it and struggle with the challenge to make the private and public personas a complete entity. You learn, over time, through the fascination and interest that friends express over you at parties, with an international identity you are somehow bigger and infinitely more interesting.

Here in America immigrants and natural born citizens are taught two primary lessons: 1) Bigger is better, and 2) Two are better than one. Like the pleasure of exotic food and drink, appreciating your ethnic background is a refined taste that some of us cultivate later, rather than earlier, in life. I, for one, have a greater appreciation, acceptance, and interest in my Danube Swabian background than ever before—and yes, it has everything to do with the benefits and personal synthesis I've received in writing this book. Admittedly, and in agreement with my mother's assessment, it's been a long time in coming. For that I offer the third American primary lesson in reply: 3) Better late than never.

PART IV

The End Peace ~ The Heal of the Bread

Henry Andor, Jr. on his wedding day.

> *"Would you go back?"*
> *"Not really. It was a hard life."*
> Maria Andor

Would you go back? I asked my mother.

"It was a nice life.... It was a simple life ... It was home ..."

But no. Unlike many people displaced from their homelands, they have no desire to return to reclaim the land. My mother gives me that run-on laugh from a private place only she knows.

"Not really," she says. "It was a hard life."

She has come to appreciate the modern conveniences of automatic dishwashing machines and fresh, store-bought bread, even while she sits in the darkness of her ranch home conserving electricity and refusing to turn on her central air conditioning until 3:00 p.m. in the scorching heat of a summer afternoon.

"The light hurts my eyes," she admonishes me when I flip the switch in exasperation on the gathering gray gloom that hovers over the kitchen and dining room tables and floats menacingly through the hallways.

"I like it a little warmer," she explains as we roast in the brick oven that is her house.

She refuses to keep the thermostat at 80 degrees and the air conditioner constantly on.

"That way you don't have to keep turning it on and off; it will do it automatically," I venture to no avail."

Automatic settings are Satan's toolbox for people who always like to be in control.

And, Mom must be in control of her personal domain. Lighting. Temperature. Piles of mail. Adult children. All that is seen and unseen. Pure. Inviolate. Impenetrable. It's safer that way. Cleaner. And definitely more manageable.

I can't ever see her moving from her home on Kilpatrick. After she hurt her back and came down with the shingles, I considered living closer to her, just in case, and I envisioned for some weeks later a two-flat or a duplex dwelling where we could be close but still have our own separate residences. Mom needs her own space. I do, too. But when I consider the fact that she only put up a garage, a deck and had the central air installed just two years ago, I think, *who am I kidding?* After 35 years in that house, she's only just moved in.

◆   ◆   ◆

I talked with my brother, Henry, today. He is home for the week watching his four children while his wife, Sharon, enjoys a much needed solo vacation at her mother's house in Steven's Point, Wisconsin. After raving on and on about the technological wonder and convenience of his new digital cellular service, we move on to the big Kahuna topic between us—*our mother.* Today we bemoan her hesitancy and caution about—well, everything really—and most specifically about her refusal yesterday to accompany Henry and his brood to Wisconsin to visit Sharon for the day.

Henry co-owns a six-seater Bonanza with two other high-flying buddies and they keep it in a hanger at the DuPage County Airport about 10 minutes from his home. It is a fine plane, and on a day like yesterday when the sky is clear and the 80-degree weather fair, it is a real joy to be up in it. When my mother called me on Tuesday to let me know that she was considering flying with Henry and the kids on Thursday, I was elated. How wonderful for my mother to experience Henry's flying on such a beautiful day. How marvelous for her to put her trust in her son's capabilities. How fabulous her effort to support him in his passion, and in so doing, exhibit a passion in her own sense of adventure. I did my best to encourage her.

On Tuesday night, she sounded so hopeful.

"Well, if I go, I'm not saying I will, but if I do, I'll go to Henry's on Wednesday night and then stay there until Friday."

I knew she was fence-sitting, but there was a youthful lilt in her voice. It made me happy imagining her face looking out over the horizon, clouds pillows for her feet.

"What is that? What is that?" she'd repeat, surveying the grids of towns below in wide-eyed wonder.

And Henry's children would point and giggle in reply.

But it was not to be.

"Oh, no." Henry says resignedly as I wander around my yard with the cordless phone in one hand and the grass edger in the other, alternating between sharpening the edges of my perception and my lawn.

"I never thought she would do it."

Henry and I commiserate about her overcautiousness.

"Do you know what she told me when I quit my job to get into flying?" 'Why do you want to do that when you have such a nice job at Bigsby and Kruthers?'

"What," Captain Henry asks, "was so nice about a $25,000 a year job selling suits for 10-12 hours a day, six-to-seven days a week?"

Henry and I are entering that special place between siblings when they finally agree on something, especially their mother.

"She hates change."

"She's a control freak."

We dig deeper yet.

"Both Mom and Dad didn't trust people," Henry says. "They kept to themselves and their friends from overseas."

He's right. They did what a lot of immigrants do. They recreated their closed, homogenous Danube Swabian cultures in America, and although they were polite with the neighbors, they kept to themselves. They were comfortable in their insulated, self-sufficiency and they expected everyone else to do the same. They asked for no help and preferred that no one ask anything of them.

"It was their way or no way," Henry continues. "I watched the way Dad did business with people. You learn how people think that way. Not by what they say, but by what they do."

My father had a reputation of being a tough negotiator, at union meetings and on the showroom floor. While Henry speaks, I can see a line of car salesmen chasing my father to the front door and my father turning around with that determined cock of his head in the days when a cash deal gave a buyer some leverage.

"I try to be very affectionate with my children," Henry tells me. "I sit them on my lap and hold them and talk to them. I have no memory of Dad ever holding me. I don't think he was capable of showing affection. He left all the emotional upbringing to Mom."

Henry adds quickly, "But that's not to say that he did not give us anything. He was a great provider. He knew how to take care of us materially."

My father took care of the basics, and the luxuries. We never did without. My memory fills suddenly with the summer vacations of my youth. Every year my father took us on fabulous vacations, one more exotic than the other. The Dells. Lake of the Ozarks. St. Petersburg, Florida. God, we all roasted in the car for three days without air conditioning. We learned how to swim in Florida at the pool at the Best Western. Then there was Mackinac Island and the Great Lakes Tour. Hiking the mountain paths in Estes Park, Colorado that haunt me to this day, urging my hasty return. Oahu, Hawaii to visit my aunt. Then Germany, Austria, Yugoslavia, and finally his birthplace, Romania.

And Mom kept us fed and clean and clothed properly, even though change is a topic she doesn't do well. In her frightened and closed heart, she would prefer us to stay stable, if moderately successful, resigned happily to mediocre, comfortable lives. But now that we are adults, support of our risk-taking is what we really need from her, more than anything else.

"The way our parents are affects us, too," Henry says knowingly. "We're distrustful and stubborn, too. We want things our own way. And, that affects our relationships with other people. In a relationship, you have to give, and be willing to receive. Relationships can't be one-sided. They have to be nurtured."

Reciprocity is a hard-won lesson for a family of control freaks.

I am having the delicious realization that my brother, who once forgot to pull a punch during some spirited childhood play fighting and gave me an impressive shiner, has wowed me again by turning into an intuitive, aware man.

Wondering aloud where he got his valuable insights, I ask, "Are you in therapy?"

"No," he laughs. "I think it has something to do with turning 40." With two years on him in this magical decade and neck deep in my own retrospective self-examination, I understand completely his thoughtful awareness and the need to observe his past for the sake of his enriching his future history.

"What else is going on?" he asks, as we try in vain to turn the conversation away from *Die Mutter*.

"I sold my house in six days, and as usual, Mom was mortified."

"You're making a big mistake," was what she said.

Henry has learned to keep his dreams to himself until he realizes them and then he presents them to her as a fait accompli. The method works; it protects him from the cold shower, and she from the anxiety of the change, but it prevents them both from sharing fully in the joyful path that is his life.

"I think she's the way she is because of what happened to her," I say, knowing full well that she'd rather see me back in a corporate job than writing this book.

There weren't many writers or artists in Kruschiwl. Farming was necessary for existence. Dreamers were not encouraged. And, then when you consider how Kruschiwl changed for her and for so many, why, anything to do with it, including writing this book, becomes a very scary proposition. Could it be that Maria is trying to protect me as well?

I keep reminding her that America has room for dreamers. Dreamers who believe the world is ready to hear her story and what happened to the Danube

Swabians. She doesn't understand or believe that, either. But that's OK. I love her anyway, and despite the fact that we have our philosophical differences of opinion, she loves me back with a blind and steady loyalty. And that, perhaps, is her greatest gift of all.

"So finish this book and get a real job," she tells me.

"And start writing the next one," I answer back.

My brother has a day at the aquarium planned with his crew, so our conversation comes to a close. As I click off the phone and put my edger back in the musty garage that smells of spilled fertilizer, I think, *what a neat man my brother has turned out to be.* And, as I close the door and return to the broad daylight of the yard, I can still hear his heavily accented, northwest-side Chicago voice.

"It a wonder, Ing, that we didn't end up really screwed up."

Maria Andor and baby daughter, Ingrid.

"Don't be ashamed of who you are.
You didn't have anything to do with it. And neither did we.
Be proud to be a German."
Maria Andor

There was a time not all that long ago—probably a year ago when I began writing this book—that I still felt some measure of responsibility over the Holocaust. In some deeply ingrained way, I believed that I was born to the most reprehensible ethnic group. Say what you will about the German sense of order and cleanliness, practicality and beer, gemuetlichkeit and wurst, polkas and waltzes, we were still all the scum of the earth. Because all of us who are born German bear the responsibility of collective guilt: the guilt by association that can never be removed. As a German, I was heir to Hitler, to the Nazis, to the beasts; I would be forever tainted by my birth.

My mother was convicted of being German at a time and in a place where it was most inopportune, and she was made to suffer the indignity of slavery. She was stripped of her citizenship rights and deemed a nonentity in the place of her birth. She was placed in a concentration camp to suffer prior to being expelled as a homeless refugee. This has not in the least been my experience when I travel abroad. But Germans are still defiled and perceived like a bad taste in the mouth. "You know, they were *German*," a Mexican innkeeper once confided to me distastefully, explaining away the rigid behavior of her least popular guests.

That World War II thing still gives us the worst of trickle-down reputations. We are not the world's most popular people.

Guilt, like water and blood, I've learned, flows from generation to generation and seeks it lowest level. If you let it, if you are not vigilant to the subtle and insidious ways it can seep into your psyche, it can find the shameful, dark canopy of your heart and live in its shadow for years. Only my guilt did not come from my mother; it came to me collectively and pressed in upon me like the broad sweep of a stereotypical generalization. *Germans are bad, distasteful barbarians,* said the tide.

For the longest time, since I was in high school, or maybe even earlier, I wanted to change my name to Anderson. *Ingrid Anderson.* I used to write it over and over the way my father wrote out his name on the notepad by the phone. It looked and sounded so good. I wanted to divorce myself of my German heritage and recreate myself as a Swede. They were more neutral during the war, and as far as I know, they are a people known for their stature and attractiveness. They enjoy a high standard of living, and aside from the Vikings, bear no 20th century reputation for getting in someone else's face. The blond hair I could get out of a bottle, I reasoned.

So often, still, when people hear my name, they automatically assume I am Swedish. Sometimes I think they really want me to be. So often I just wanted to say in an upbeat, you guessed it right kind of way, *yeah, yes, I'm Swedish,* instead of *no, I'm German,* with a somewhat subdued and apologetic downward cast to my eyes.

Was it too many Holocaust movies? Too many stereotypically evil Germans? I'm a gray person by nature and all I got growing up was black and white. Jews are victims and Germans are villains. The good guys and the bad guys. Over and over the litany rang in my ears. 'The world must never forget.' *Germans must never be forgiven.* And this feeling of self-hatred over one's pathetic ethnicity must pass down to every generation, in much the same way as the Russians invaded Czechoslovakia and took joy in murdering the Sudetenland babies and pregnant women. 'The German beast must be stopped in the womb,' so the propagandists said.

No matter how often my mother turned off the TV, I still grew up inundated with negative ethnic images in all popular media. There was no other choice but to assume I was associated with a race of jack-booted, snarling, black-lipped beasts. It wasn't until Steven Spielberg produced Schindler's List that my black and white, victim and villain palette suddenly faded to gray. At last, someone attempted to show the complexity of the human condition. We are not all bad; we are not all good. We are somewhere in between. And here are two men—a German named Schindler and a Jew named Spielberg—to prove it.

Prior to Schindler's List, I developed a media-induced shame, responsibility, and guilt over something that was not my fault. Nor, I realize now, were my parents to blame. In point of fact, if you subscribe to the theory that Germans as a whole are an accursed race and have a price to pay, my parents and the Danube

Swabians more than paid theirs. So why, until the writing of this book, wasn't I able to feel some level of absolution?

There is still this insidious victim mentality that runs through our society. And, as long as we support a victim identity from generation to generation, from family to family, we must also support a perpetrator identity, as well. The one needs the other to exist. In this world it seems there must always be one to be pitied and one to bear the blame.

When does the victim mentality stop? When does the perpetrator identity stop? When do you turn the prism and allow the healing to begin? When it can be said and put into words with true belief behind them, it can become reality. Just like my thoughts, my dreams, and this book.

This is the hardest part of the book for me to write because it's the ending. I've been hanging on to this guilt like I've been avoiding finishing the book proposal like I've been running away from ending this book. But that's really where we are now. That's where all this had led. My mother's martyrdom is long past. She is my hero. I have safe passage now as I have always had with her.

"Don't be silly," she says to me about feeling the collective German angst. "Don't be ashamed of who you are. You didn't have anything to do with it. And neither did we. You have nothing to be ashamed about. Be proud to be a German."

My mother has this predictably simple and straightforward manner about her that is both comforting and daunting, all at the same time.

I don't know if I'm up for a German Pride Day yet, but I can say that I've let go of the guilt. I'm not buying into it anymore. Somehow I took it on and somehow I'm taking it off. It doesn't belong on my shoulders and it never did. It's not my legacy. I suspect there aren't very many people alive anymore who should be wearing the collective guilt mantle, and I'm all for a collective unfurling. My advice to anyone out there still suffering: Give it up. You can't change history and you're not responsible. Don't take everything you see or hear so literally. It's not the whole truth; it's just a portion. Reality is much more complex, much more gray. And, so are the people. And, the circumstances.

I learned something very important while writing this book. I discovered it somewhere in the silence between the tears and frustrations of those doomed to be unpopular, unacknowledged victims, and from those whose voices cry out from the pages of witness. We are all victims. We are all villains. We are unequal parts victim and villain, with different times and circumstances pitting us more to one side or the other. We are mirror images unto ourselves. People across the globe, throughout the centuries, from every race and creed, have suffered and caused others to do the same. And, in our darkness, we will probably continue to do so from one horrifying degree to another.

Germans are, and were, Hitler's victims, too. The ethnic Germans who suffered in the concentration camps of eastern Europe. The Nazi supporters, who were beguiled by fear and intimidation. The modern-day nationals, who had nothing to do with the second World War, who continue to make public apologies for the actions of their forbears. And, others, like me, first generation American kids who grow up guilty and confused, despite their parent's good intentions. We are all victims of the hype. I say: It's time to throw off the jackboots and pull down the swastikas. Enough of it already.

◆   ◆   ◆

March, 1999

Stop. Rewind. I wish it were so easy. But I have to stop and rewind and rephrase a bit. Because even this compromise of good and evil doesn't satisfy me anymore. As an explanation, it's too pat, too limited, and doesn't contribute one iota toward changing a paradigm of thought. For if I can't offer something that will alter the narrow way we think about ourselves, as being guilty or innocent, worthy or damned, or even stranger still, partly so, then what in heaven's name has this been all about?

Can it be possible that we are neither victim nor villain? That neither existence is real? That we are something else entirely, and that in our delusion of good versus evil duality, we have completely overlooked our common heritage?

Many of us, including myself, have chosen to react to a collective consciousness in which we allow ourselves to be identified as victim or victimizer. Neither of these roles are we truly comfortable in assuming. Like actors on a stage, these are the roles we have chosen to play. But they are not representative of who we really are. Instead of recognizing our vast potential, and casting aside the roles of victim and victimizer, we have taught them to our children, passing along the identities others have projected onto us. They are but projections of fear, and to define ourselves in these limited ways does each of us a disservice. When do we finally put aside our masks and let the curtain rise on our true identities?

Over the centuries, humankind has been on a teeter-totter of misery, alternating between projection and finger-pointing. However, on a teeter-totter, there is that point where we can shift ourselves far enough forward or lean far enough back: that point where we hover in perfect balance and look evenly into each other's eyes. And, then, when the fog in our mirror clears and we can see our own reflection, who is left to blame and who to bear it? How can we be victim and villain, guilty and guiltless, as one?

There still exists this resistance to greatness and transcendence; as in the pecking order of victims, there still exists a competition among those who suffered. Which battle exacted more casualties? Whose crimes were more heinous? In the final analysis of agony, no one really cares save the ego, which seeks to separate and carve differences to feed its own fears. For is not ethnocentrism, the belief that one ethnic group is better than another—nay all *isms* which promote one's superiority at the expense of another—are they not all of the ego? And, therefore, a denial of the self? And, is not the belief in unity—that we are all equally deserving of love—is that not of the heart, the place of acceptance, the very church bell within our core that rings true? What good, then, is superiority at the expense of isolation? Or silence as a substitute for awareness? What value is there in hiding?

As the Romans laid the groundwork before them, Hitler had his Himmler to crucify the Jews as Tito had his Pijade to crucify the ethnic Germans. And there have been emulators in other lands and other times whose crimes and faces blend one into the other. In the end, are they not all extreme examples of how we choose to crucify ourselves each and every day?

Let us cast aside these false roles that we have made to limit us, and instead accept the magnitude of our existence. Rather than the crucifixion, let us seek the resurrection. Instead of the darkness, let us turn to the light. And, like the bread, let us rise to our birthright and live in the true consciousness of who we really are—and how we were always intended to be—guiltless, glorious sons and daughters of God.

I'm free now, Mother. Thank you.

Maria Andor at Das Haus der Donauschwaben in Sindelfingen, Germany.

Afterword

"Yes, Mother, I remember."

Lufthansa Flight LH432 to Chicago—April 22, 1999

It began for me in San Miguel de Allende two years ago under a clear blue cloudless sky in a colonial Silver City in central Mexico and it ended two years later under a cold rainy gray sky in Sindelfingen, Germany at the House of the Donauschwaben on April 17, 1999. My mother and I came to Germany for this particular event in Sindelfingen: to attend the reunion of the survivors of the concentration camp that was erected in 1944 in my mother's home town of Kruschiwl, Yugoslavia. We are here with my mother's first cousins, Eva and Michael, whose lives also began in Kruschiwl before the Second World War.

In the House of the Donauschwaben, just down the street from the Mercedes Benz corporate offices in Sindelfingen, there is a room filled with pictures taken of the towns and the fields where the Donauschwaben lived and worked in the Batschka and Banat regions in Yugoslavia and Romania. At the head of each orderly culdesac of pictures stand a pair of cheerful, lifeless department store dummies wearing the voluminous pleated skirts of the women's ethnic costume and the severe black pants and vest belonging to the men. At the far end, just over one dummy's right shoulder and behind the full-size antique horse drawn wagon that pulled a family of refugees to safety in Germany, is a glass display case in which a scaled down prototype of Kruschiwl stands. One main street, two side streets, a railroad track that leads on to the next town, and beyond that, the fields. My mother and I and her cousins gather together at the prototype and gaze down at what can only be described as a very small town.

"Remember, I told you, that's the track we used to get our beets and grain out to the factories," my mother reminds me.

"Yes, mother, I remember," I reply to her questioning gaze.

Eva, my mother's cousin, moves over behind the display case where the church stands in the middle of the long main street. I join her there and watch her index finger move over three places.

"We lived in this house," she tells me, pointing, "three houses from the church." And moving to the fourth house, she turns her head in my direction and adds, "This is where your mother lived."

Except for this prototype of Kruschiwl and the sensory memory it leaves in the lives of its previous inhabitants, Kruschiwl no longer exists, not even this church; for it, too, like most of the houses after the Serbians colonized it, was eventually dismantled, brick by brick. Like the few bricks that may yet litter the dusty road that was once the main street of this town, there are also few people remaining who once led peaceful farming lives there.

Of the 950 people who lived in Kruschiwl, 250 townspeople died there in the camp, and only 70 of the remaining survivors have made it to the reunion. I move to the presentation room to sit with them and we listen to the speakers who recall the history of the settlement and the tragedy of the expulsion. We pray the *Vater Unser* (Our Father) and lay a wreath at the memorial wall in the garden outside. Together, we remember those who died in the camps, and in Russia, and we remind ourselves quietly that, yes, it really did happen, and that, yes, we were really all there just as surely as we are here today, even if my mother's passport does not bear the now nonexistent place of her birth.

On the way to Sindelfingen, in fact, everywhere I go in Germany, Kosovo hangs over us like a big, foreboding, yet strangely familiar cloud. Like the weather, dark and patchy, intermittent rain showers break forth and the talk bounces around me, like bullets in the car. It and the talk of "what happened to us in Kruschiwl 55 years ago" meet like a hot and cold front, and the din rings in my ears.

"Milosevic and the Serbs...."

"Just like Tito and the partisans ..."

"Look what happened to us...."

I watch the windshield wipers momentarily wipe the raindrops away, and for a blessed moment, I wish I could do the same to the talk inside the car.

Kosovo has followed me to every sitting at every table in every house in which I have been a guest. It has been my companion to the left, beside my fork, in the frustrated voice of my mother's cousin Michael; to the right, beside my knife, in the voice that is my mother's, the one that no longer trusts; and across the table, over the Kuchen and the strudel, high above the coffee pot, in the flushed, young, angry face of my cousin Wolfgang. The sound of Kosovo is the sound of frustration is the sound of the refugee is the sound of helplessness and it lingers around me like a guest whose welcome has long ago worn thin.

The men become agitated and frustrated, agreeing that the NATO bombing was the wrong move and *nutzt nichts* (was useless). There is some discussion of assassinating Milosevic, if they could only find him; but it, like all of it, is just talk and no one has any viable answers to the conflict. The futility of discussing the whys and wherefores of this political cesspool frustrates me, too, but I remain patient and try not to engage or provoke any additional conversation. For, after all, I am here to remember Kruschiwl, not Kosovo; but for me, like them, the similarity of the situation has not gone unnoticed.

While the air war in Kosovo rages on and the tired, bedraggled refugees stream across the Serbian border, I sit with the few surviving refugees of Kruschiwl, Yugoslavia—victims of another Serbian ethnic cleansing carried out 55 long, lonely years ago. Unlike you, most of the world does not know their story. Many of the books on refugees and genocide do not count the Donauschwaben among them. And now, with their numbers dwindling, not many are left who can tell it.

At 59, Michael, my first cousin once removed, is the youngest survivor represented in Sindelfingen. When he was six years old, his grandfather was privileged to receive a well-timed tip from a partisan guard. This partisan informed him that on the following morning when the drum roll would sound, the children would be taken out of the camp and placed in Serbian children's orphanages. Michael's grandfather knew he had to make a snap decision. That night, while the guards that manned the perimeter around their house came together to talk, they inadvertently opened up an escape route and Michael's grandfather, grandmother, and 15-year-old sister, Eva, smuggled Michael out of the concentration camp that my mother was still in, and through the night they walked over the border to Hungary. Like the Albanian refugees today, they ultimately found their way to Germany—where they were also not wanted—and made new lives in Griesheim, near Darmstadt, a town south of Frankfurt that was settled and built by Donauschwaben refugees like themselves.

This week, according to the newscasts, Germany has again reluctantly agreed to do its part in the Kosovo crisis by accepting 10,000 Albanian refugees. Fifty-five years ago, after Germany quaked in fear and allowed a madman to run amok and create a world crisis in which millions of people were displaced—including the Donauschwaben from their eastern European homelands—Germany was forced to accept millions more. At that time, unlike Germany's efficient and productive present, its economic engine had had its gears stripped and its breadbasket lay barren. Each day in cities like Munich and Dresden and Frankfurt and Berlin, hundreds of thousands of starving, homeless refugees streamed into its bombed cities with horse drawn wagons—like the one I saw in Sindelfin-

gen—children strapped into wheelbarrows and mothers picking through the garbage for scraps. Look into the faces of the Albanians and you will see my mother,
my father, my grandmother, my grandfather, my aunts, my uncles, and my cousins, too.

Today Germany can easily accept the 10,000 Albanian refugees and probably
more. And, so can the other neighboring European countries, as well as the U.S.
We all need to help each other in this current crisis, just like the world had to
help over 50 years ago and in all the times when a loose screw rolls precariously
over the factory floor.

Comparisons are not really necessary. Nor are they welcome or important. All
I hear is just the recurring litany of history repeating itself. The gong sounds out
the years and the death tolls:

1915-1917	800,000 Armenians
1929-1939	20,000,000 Soviets
1933-1945	6,000,000 Jews
1944-1948	2,000,000 Danube Swabians
1971	3,000,000 Bangladeshis
1972-1975	100,000 Hutu.

And, that just includes some of the high points in 20th century genocide.
Genocide can be linked to the names of Hitler, Stalin, Tito, Milosevic, Pol Pot,
and countless others whose names are lost to me, but whose ancient legacy of
hatred lives on. The years, the names, the faces all fade into one terrifying, yet
recognizable mass. Time is not really time here. In this place, time has not really
past. It will not appear again in the future. For it is all happening in the same
augenblick (blink of an eye)—the present eternity constantly occurring over and
over again. No answers as to what causes genocide and the expulsion and dis-
placement of refugees the world over. Proof only that we seem to hate our brothers with the same fervor as we hate ourselves.

This morning, on my last day in Germany, I sat at a kitchen table, lingering
over my very American breakfast of Kellogg's corn flakes and bananas. My
mother's cousins in-law, an elderly couple, rode over on their bicycles to bid us a
fond farewell. Within moments of their arrival, the talk, as its always does,
returned to Kosovo. I hear my mother, like many of the Donauschwaben refugees who were victims of Tito and Hitler 55 years ago, say that she doesn't trust

Milosevic or any Serb, and that she does not understand why he wants to clear Kosovo of its Albanian population.

"What does he want to do?" she asks in wonder, musing about his colonization plans. "Who does he want to put there? Who will settle those lands now?"

I know she is thinking about Kruschiwl and the Serbian colonists who were given her home. I wonder if she remembers the history of her ancestors' immigration: that it was the defeat and expulsion of the Turks in the 1700's by the Austria-Hungary Empire that created the colonization opportunities for her ancestors in the first place. God, we could go even farther back to Alexander the Great and his exploits in that part of the world.

When has ethnic cleansing ever made any sense, I want to say, but bite my tongue and leave the table to ready myself to take my daily walk in the woods of Griesheim and my leave of Germany. The woods, silent save for the reassuring sounds of birds, seem to me to be the safest, most peaceful place on this very normal, uneventful day when I will leave my past behind.

From a distance while I linger by the front door, I hear the old man ask my mother about life in Chicago. Of all the things he could possibly say, I overhear his question and inwardly cringe.

"Do you have Blacks living near you?"

Not wanting to hear my mother's answer, I open the door and think, *Oh God, will we never learn? How many of these opportunities will we continuously miss?* I look about me, my head raised to another cloudy April sky that threatens rain, and take a deep breath of fresh air, closing the door on Kosovo—and Kruschiwl—for the last time.

About the Author

Back row from left: Eva Zettl Anile, Katharina Szettele Gronner, Eva Halblaender,
Ingrid Andor, Katharina Ruscheinski, Michael Zettl, Katharina Burlem, Adam Szettele.
Front row from left: Albert Zettl, Jakob Zettl, Maria Andor, Rosalia Szettele, and Christine Kiefer.

Ingrid Andor is a proud member of the children of immigrants born in America. She is hard at work, completing the circle of gratitude and returning the favor so graciously given to her own parents when they came to this country. After many years in corporate marketing communications and product administration, Ingrid obtained a master's degree in linguistics so she could help immigrants with their English language learning. Ingrid teaches academic reading and writing skills to ESL students in Chicago.

Notes

Notes to Part I

1. Estimates of Swabians in Yugoslavia reported in *A Terrible Revenge: The Ethnic Cleansing of the East European Germans, 1944-1950,* (New York: St. Martin's Press, 1994), 95.

2. Czech occupation reported in *A Terrible Revenge: The Ethnic Cleansing of the East European Germans, 1944-1950,* (New York: St. Martin's Press, 1994), 90.

3. Methgethen and Nemmersdorf incidents reported in *A Terrible Revenge: The Ethnic Cleansing of the East European Germans, 1944-1950,* (New York: St. Martin's Press, 1994), 35-47.

4. Sea disasters reported in *Nemesis at Postdam: The Anglo-Americans and the Expulsion of the Germans: Background, Execution, Consequence,* (London: Routledge & Kegan Paul Ltd., 1977), 73-75.

Notes to Part II

5. Killing of orphans in sugar refinery reported in "The Genocide of the Indigenous Ethnic Germans of Yugoslavia (1944-1948) and the Deliberate Media Cover-up" in *Nachrichten,* Vol. 45, 9, (Chicago: Vereinigung der Donauschwaben, 1999), 7.

Notes to Part III

6. Immigration issues reported in *United States Policy on Immigration: An Overview of the Issues Affecting the Immigration Policy of the United States,* (Kansas: The University of Kansas National Textbook Publishing Company, 1994), 56.

7.   Immigration issues reported in "Closed Borders: The Contemporary Assault on Freedom of Movement," *A Twentieth Century Fund Report,* (New Haven: Yale University Press, 1987), 102.

Bibliography

Bresser, Michael. "History of the Danube Swabians in the USA." In *Nachrichten*. Vol. 5. Chicago: Vereinigung der Donauschwaben, 2000.

De Zayas, Alfred-Maurice. *A Terrible Revenge: The Ethnic Cleansing of the East European Germans, 1944-1950*. New York: St. Martin's Press, 1994.

De Zayas, Alfred-Maurice. *Nemesis at Potsdam: The Anglo-Americans and the Expulsion of the Germans. Background, Execution, Consequences*. London: Routledge & Kegan Paul Ltd., 1997.

Dowty, Alan. "Closed Borders: The Contemporary Assault on Freedom of Movement." A Twentieth Century Fund Report. New Haven: Yale University Press, 1987.

Genocide of the Ethnic Germans in Yugoslavia 1944-1948. Chicago: Danube Swabian Association of the USA., 2001.

Rowland, Robert C. *United States Policy on Immigration: An Overview of the Issues Affecting the Immigration Policy of the United States*. Kansas: University of Kansas, 1994.

Schmidt, Frank. *An Introduction to the Danube Swabians*. Canada: Heimat Publishers, 1996.

Schmidt, Frank. *The Extermination of a People: A Cover-Up Uncovered*. Canada: Heimat Publishers, 1991.

Schmidt, Frank. "The Genocide of the Indigenous Ethnic Germans of Yugoslavia (1944-1948) and the Deliberate Media Cover-up." In *Nachrichten*. Vol. 45, 9. Chicago: Vereinigung der Donauschwaben, 1999.

978-0-595-46672-6
0-595-46672-9

63469945R00115

Made in the USA
Lexington, KY
08 May 2017